Sports Law in The Netherlands

Sports Law in The Netherlands

Second Edition

Steven F.H. Jellinghaus
Jolande M.M. Janssen
Dennis Schwartz
Harry van Drongelen

This book was originally published as a monograph in the International Encyclopaedia of Laws/Sports Law.

Founding Editor: Roger Blanpain
General Editor: Frank Hendrickx
Volume Editor: Michele Colucci

Wolters Kluwer

Published by:
Kluwer Law International B.V.
PO Box 316
2400 AH Alphen aan den Rijn
The Netherlands
E-mail: international-sales@wolterskluwer.com
Website: www.wolterskluwer.com/en/solutions/kluwerlawinternational

Sold and distributed by:
Wolters Kluwer Legal & Regulatory U.S.
7201 McKinney Circle
Frederick, MD 21704
United States of America
E-mail: customer.service@wolterskluwer.com

ISBN 978-94-035-4125-9

e-Book: ISBN 978-94-035-4130-3
web-PDF: ISBN 978-94-035-4131-0

The Authors

Steven F.H. Jellinghaus, is a leading authority in the field of employee participation and sports law in the Netherlands. As a lawyer, arbitrator, author and lecturer on sports law and labour law at Tilburg University, the Netherlands, he is active in all facets of labour law and sports law. He obtained a PhD on the harmonization of working conditions, and he is a member of various (sport related) supervisory boards, project groups and committees. He is the author of the renowned book on sports law: *Capita Sportrecht* and editorial member of *Tijdschrift voor Sport en Recht (Magazine on Sports law).*

Jolande M.M. Janssen is an expert at the intersection of employee participation, corporate law and labour law, in particular, mergers, takeovers, financing, restructuring and social plans, and also active in the field of sports law and health care law. She has written the client counsels manual 'Handboek voor Cliëntenraden' and acts as a committee member on various dispute committees.

The Authors

Dennis Schwartz, Lawyer at De Voort Advocaten | Mediators is specialized in (collective) labour law and sports law. He is a regularly published author on those subjects, board member of several disputes committees and board member of the disciplinary committee of the Royal Dutch Swimming Association. He is also chairman of the oldest sports club in his home town Maarssen; *MZ&PC De Fuut.*

Harry van Drongelen, born at The Hague in 1952, studied Law at Leiden University, the Netherlands. He graduated in Civil Law in 1979 and obtained a general degree in Law in 1981. In 1991, he obtained his doctorate at Maastricht University, the Netherlands, with a dissertation on 'The Development of the Labour Inspectorate in a Changing Legislation'. He has worked as legislator at the Ministry of Social Affairs and was Associate Professor on Social Law and Social Policy at Tilburg University, the Netherlands. He regularly publishes in his areas of expertise.

Table of Contents

List of Abbreviations

BVO	*Betaald voetbalorganisatie* (Professional Football Organization)
BW	*Burgerlijk Wetboek* (Civil Code)
CBS	*Centraal bureau voor de statistiek* (Dutch Central Statistical Office)
CLA	Collective Labour Agreement
CNV	*Christelijke Nederlandse Vakbeweging* (National Federation of Christian Trade Unions)
CRvB	*Centrale Raad van Beroep* (Dutch Central Appeals Tribunal (Social Security Law))
FBO	*Federatie van Betaald Voetbal Organisaties* (Federation of Professional Football Organizations)
HR	*Hoge Raad* (Dutch Supreme Court)
ISR	*Instituut voor Sport Rechtspraak* (Institute for Sport Adjudication)
JAR	*Jurisprudentie Arbeidsrecht* (Case Law Labour Law)
JIN	*Jurisprudentie in Nederland* (Case Law)
KNVB	*Koninklijke Nederlandse Voetbalbond* (Royal Dutch Football Association)
KNZB	*Koninklijke Nederlandse Zwembond* (Royal Dutch Swimming Association)
NJ	*Nederlandse jurisprudentie* (Dutch Case Law)
NOC*NSF	*Nationaal Olympisch comitee Nederlandse sport federatie* (National Olympic Committee * The Netherlands Sports Federation)
RV	*Wetboek voor rechtsvordering* (Code of Civil Proceedings)
TvSR	*Tijdschrift voor Sport en Recht* (Journal on Sports Law)
USZ	*Uitspraak sociale zekerheid* (Social Security Case Law)
UWV	*Uitvoeringsinstituut Werknemersverzekeringen*

List of Abbreviations

WAVV	*Wet algemeen verbindend verklaring* (Act on the Declaration of the Universally Binding and Non-binding Status of Collective Labour Agreements)
WIA	*Wet Inkomen en Arbeid* (Income and Ability to Work Act)
WOR	*Wet op de ondernemingsraden* (Works Council Act)
WUAB	*Wet uitvoering antidopingbeleid* (Law on Execution of the Anti-doping Policy)

Foreword

Sport has a unique position in the law as a result of the legal complexity which arises from self-regulation of sports associations. This monograph intends to unravel this complexity with regard to company law, labour law, disciplinary law, dispute resolution and portrait rights. On the other hand, it is not the intention of this monograph to discuss the entire field of, for example, Dutch labour law. For further information on that area, we refer the reader to the already existing publications on this subject by the authors. This update includes the parts on disciplinary law and dispute resolution.

Tilburg, August 2021

Steven F.H. Jellinghaus
S.jellinghaus@devoort.nl/S.F.H.Jellinghaus@tilburguniversity.edu
Jolande M.M. Janssen
J.Janssen@devoort.nl
Dennis Schwartz
D.schwartz@devoort.nl
Harry van Drongelen
vdrongel@xs4all.nl

General Introduction

Chapter 1. Sports in the Netherlands

1. Many people practice sports in the Netherlands.[1] Studies show that the number of people practising sports weekly is stable as shown in Figure 1.

Figure 1 People Practising Sports Weekly

The number of people practising sports weekly (2001–2019) by the Dutch Population:

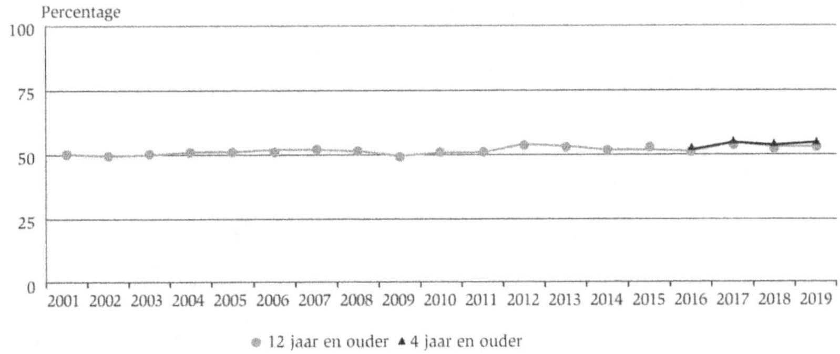

1. *Source: website* https://www.sportenbewegenincijfers.nl/kernindicatoren/sportdeelname-wekelijks en CBS-Gezondheidsenquête (2001-2013), Gezondheidenquête/Leefstijlmonitor CBS i.s.m het RIVM (2014-2018) en Gezondheidsmonitor Volwassenen en Ouderen 2016 GGD'en, CBS en RIVM.

The number of people practising sports weekly based on age (2001–2019) by the Dutch population:

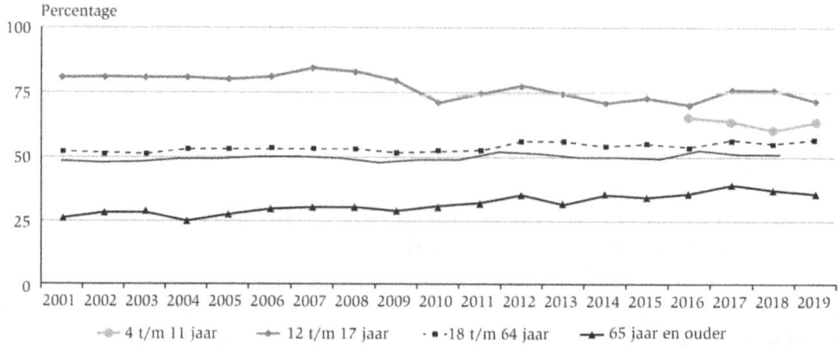

Approximately half of the people who practise sports are members of sports clubs as shown in Figure 2.

Figure 2 Of Those Who Practise Sport, the Percentage Who Belong to Sporting

Clubs 2012–2018[2]

The percentages of people practising sports divided into the different branches of sports are listed in Table 1.

2. 6 years and older *Source: website:* https://www.sportenbewegenincijfers.nl/kernindicatoren/clublidmaatschapen *Vrijetijdsomnibus (VTO) Sociaal en Cultureel Planbureau (SCP Sociaal Cultureel Planbureau) in samenwerking met het CBS, 2012–2018.*

Table 1 Percentage of Practitioners of Sports Divided into the Different Branches[3]

Year	*Fitness*	*Jogging/Running*	*Soccer*	*Swimming*	*Tennis*	*Hockey*	*Volleyball*
2001	14.3	5.1	7.5	13	9.6	1.1	3.1
2002	15	5.9	7.1	12.6	9.9	1.5	5.7
2003	17.8	6.8	7.6	9.7	9.4	1.5	3.1
2004	18	6.7	8	8.6	8.5	1.3	2.6
2005	19.6	7.3	7.1	8.1	8.4	1.3	2.8
2006	19.3	7.7	8	7.8	8	1.8	2.5
2007	22.1	8.1	7.4	7.4	8.1	1.5	2.4
2008	22.5	7.5	7.2	7.2	8.1	1.9	2.4
2009	21.8	9.2	7.1	6.8	8.4	1.4	2.1
2010	20.5	9.9	5.3	6.7	7.6	1	2.2
2011	20.4	9.9	5.2	6.2	7.5	1	2.1
2012	23	12.5	5.4	6.8	6.9	1.3	1.9
2013	23.6	13.8	5.4	5.6	6.7	1.2	1.5
2014	22.6	13.6	7	5.6	5.9	1.5	1.7
2015	23.8	12.7	6.6	5.1	5.6	1.8	1.7
2016	23.8	12.9	6.6	5.6	5.1	1.8	1.4
2017	24.6	11.4	6.5	6.1	5.5	1.5	1.6
2018	25.1	11.8	6.4	5.8	5.4	1.9	1.4
2019	22.6	10.7	7.7	5.8	5.1	1.3	1.3

3. https://www.sportenbewegenincijfers.nl/kernindicatoren.

Year	*Fitness*	*Jogging/Running*	*Soccer*	*Swimming*	*Tennis*	*Hockey*	*Volleyball*
Year	*Yoga*	*Golfing*	*Cycle Racing*	*Horseback Riding*	*Dancing*	*Squash*	*Skating*
2001	1.4	1.5	0.3	2.3	1.4	1.9	2.2
2002	0.8	1.7	0.4	2.5	1.6	1.8	1.8
2003	1.2	1.5	0.4	2.1	1.6	1.9	1.3
2004	1.4	1.6	0.5	2.4	1.6	1.8	1.5
2005	1.4	1.8	0.5	2.5	1.7	1.5	1
2006	1.6	1.7	0.3	2.1	1.9	1.3	0.9
2007	1.6	1.8	0.6	1.7	1.7	1.5	1
2008	1.5	2	0.6	1.9	1.5	1.4	0.6
2009	1.5	2.3	0.7	2.3	2.4	1.3	0.7
2010	1.6	3.7	1,2	1.8	1.8	1.2	0.8
2011	2	3.5	1.1	1.6	1.7	0.9	0.7
2012	2	2.3	1.1	1.5	1.9	0.9	0.7
2013	2.1	2	1.1	1.7	1.7	0.8	0.6
2014	2.2	2.2	1.5	2.1	1	0.9	0.6
2015	2.9	2.3	2.3	1.5	1.1	0.8	0.3
2016	2.5	2.3	1.8	1.9	1.4	0.8	0.5
2017	3	2	1.8	1.6	1.2	0.7	0.3
2018	3	2	1.8	1.6	1.2	0.8	0.2
2019	3.1	1.6	1.7	1.8	1.7	0.5	0.6

2. The figures above show that sports participation in the Netherlands increased between 1999 and 2019. Furthermore, the number of people who join a sporting club has decreased. These results apply to men as well as to women. Sports that can be practised alone and have a recreational nature are among the most popular sports. These sports include, among others, swimming, fitness, cycling and jogging. Hockey, golf and jogging are sports that have gained more popularity in the past few years. Soccer is ranked sixth in the national ranking, but it is the most popular team sport in the Netherlands. The KNVB (Royal Dutch Soccer Association) is by far the largest sporting association with more than 1 million members.[4] A small portion of these members, approximately 650–700, play soccer professionally. These players are employed in one of the thirty-six professional football organizations (BVO).

A growing part of the Dutch population believes that practising sports is a necessary part of a healthy lifestyle. Sports (competition) results and rankings were an important source of national pride in 2004. The Dutch professional sportsmen do perform better now than in the past. During the past fifteen years, sport results have been on the rise. The Netherlands can now be ranked somewhere between the eighth and eighteenth place in the international sports ranking; the place in the ranking depends on the criteria used.

4. In 2020 there were 1,179,933 members, according to www.knvb.nl.

Chapter 2. Development of Sports Law

3. Sports law can be seen as an interdisciplinary area of the law as there are many areas of law which impact sports. These include labour law, criminal law, commercial law and civil law. Furthermore, Dutch sports policy is influenced by the regulations of the European Union (EU) and the regional and global sporting associations. Most of the regional and global sporting associations are established in Switzerland and therefore the regulations created by these organizations are based on Swiss law. The important role of the EU regulations reflects the fact that sports law has started to play an important role in European policy. As there are no specific provisions for sports law, the general EU law should be applied to sports law issues.

4. In the Netherlands, there are (mostly) no specific rules for sports law. Only doping has a special code in which rules on this subject are laid down. One must turn to general law of the Netherlands to solve (legal) problems arising in the area of sports. However, in 2002 a collective labour agreement (CLA) for employees in the sports sector like trainers and coaches was signed, followed in 2003 by a CLA (cao) for professional sportsmen as well. The latest CLA has a duration until 31 December 2020. Since 2002, there have been several CLAs for various sports disciplines, such as football and professional cycling. In 2017, a new CLA was signed for general sports disciplines. Such as cao Sport, cao Sportverenigingen, cao Beroepsrenners, cao Betaald voetbal, etc. These agreements contain provisions specifically written for labour agreements in the area of sports. For instance, a professional sportsman's employment contract may be terminated when there is the possibility for a sportive improvement such as playing for a higher-ranked club in the Netherlands, playing in a higher-ranked competition (worldwide) or a major salary improvement. Further, this collective agreement contains special provisions for professional sportsmen in the Dutch social security system.

5. Some interesting developments have occurred in the past years. First of all, the Department of Health, Welfare and Sport created a policy report about sport. This report contains the main sport policy of the Dutch government for the period 2006–2016. In general, it creates a broad approach so that sporting organizations, governmental and educational agencies, as well as minority organizations and research institutions can be reached through this policy.

Second, a committee called 'Goed Sportbestuur' (Good Sports Governance) was created. This committee created a set of rules which sets forth in which way boards of sports clubs should conduct themselves. The Dutch government has started funding a new research programme in 2017 which ran until 2020 to stimulate research on enhancing sport performance in professional sports, research on ways to help people sport their entire life and research on the value of sport in society.

Furthermore, there has been some discussion about the lowering of legal requirements for the naturalization of professional sportsmen. On special occasions and under specific circumstances, these sportsmen can obtain Dutch citizenship even if they do not meet the general requirements set forth in Article 8 Rijkswet op het Nederlanderschap (Statute for the Dutch Nationality), if they can prove that, by their naturalization, the Dutch national interests are served. A well-known example is the so-called *Kalou* case.[5] Kalou was a soccer player who wanted to participate in the Dutch national team. The government did not accept his naturalization request, because he was not fully integrated into Dutch society, which was considered an important argument, because a professional soccer player is regarded as a role model in society.

The last remarkable development relates to the European General Data Protection Regulation (GDPR) which has sports clubs puzzled about what data they are allowed to collect from their members and under which circumstances they are allowed to do so.[6] Recently the Royal Dutch Tennis Association (KNTLB) has been fined over half a million euros by the Dutch privacy authority(Autoriteit Persoonsgegevens) for providing personal data of their members to some of their sponsors who sell sports equipment commercially.[7]

5. ABRvS 15 Feb. 2006, LJN: 1833.
6. S. Jansen, van het NK naar het EK: van nationale privacy wetgeving naar de Algemene verordening gegevensbescherming, Tijdschrift voor Sport Recht, 2017, 2/3.
7. Besluit tot het opleggen van een bestuurlijke boete, 20 Dec. 2019, Autoriteit Persoonsgegevens.

Part I. Organization of Sports

Chapter 1. General Issues

§1. Introduction

6. Sports play an important role in the day-to-day business in the Netherlands considering the number of sports associations and the number of members. At government level, responsibility for sports policy lies with the Ministry of Health, Welfare and Sports[8] and the responsibility for sports, in particular, lies with the State Secretary. An estimated 4–5 million Dutch people are members of a sports association, which constitutes approximately 30% of the total Dutch population. However, the total number of sports participants is much higher, since many people practice sports independently and are therefore not affiliated with any sports association. Over 50% of the Dutch population in the age between 15 and 75 years practice sports once a week with an average duration of one hour and twenty minutes a week. This makes sports the fourth most popular way of spending leisure time and the most popular form of outdoor recreation. Soccer is the most popular sport in the Netherlands and over a million people are affiliated with a football club. But individual sports, such as fitness, are popular as well, since people are nowadays more and more caught up in their work and social life and want to have flexibility in deciding when to practice sports. As a result of this, fitness clubs with cheap memberships have sprung up like mushrooms in comparison to the 'traditional' sports clubs:[9]

8. www.minvws.nl.
9. CBS 2017; NOC*NSF 2017. Sportonderzoek voor beleid en samenleving Mulier Instituut 2019.

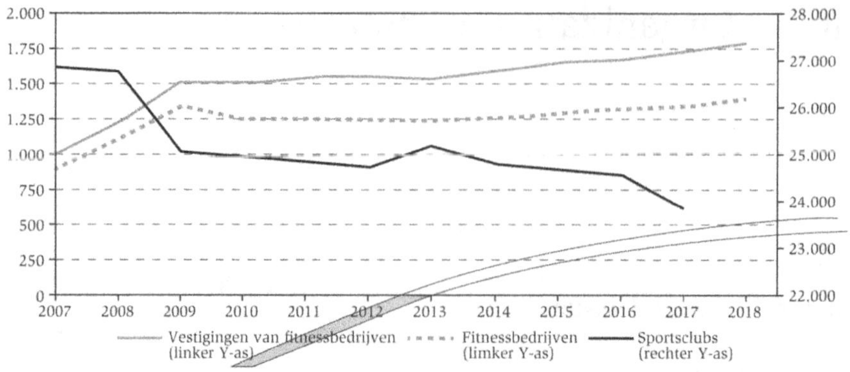

7. The role of federations, especially the role of the Dutch football federation (KNVB),[10] has been the motor of the process of professionalizing sports in the Netherlands. These federations are operating independently. All these federations have joined forces under the umbrella organization called National Olympic Committee * The Netherlands Sports Federation (NOC*NSF). This is an independent entity with its own policy. Its main task is to ensure that the Netherlands is well represented at the Olympic Games and to make sure that central government sports policy is implemented. It has established a national sports deal to stimulate sports for everybody. Other important organizations which shape the Dutch sporting landscape are the Netherlands Institute for Sports and Physical Activity (NISB),[11] the Association of Dutch Municipalities (VNG)[12] and the Association of Sports and Municipalities (VSG).[13] Furthermore there are organizations that represent coaches and ensure sportsmen–students receive proper education while being able to pursue a sports career.[14] The government's policy is to exercise supervision from afar and is, therefore, primarily one of coordination and encouragement. Therefore, not much legislation has been adopted with respect to sports.[15] The year 1954 marked the introduction of paid football, but it was not until 1967 that the agreement between a club and a professional player was recognized as an employment contract. This has significantly ameliorated the position of professionals with respect to loan and bonus agreements and is an example of the special (legal) status sports have in the Netherlands.

10. www.knvb.nl.
11. www.nisb.nl.
12. www.vng.nl.
13. www.vsg.nl.
14. Example, VSG or KVLO.
15. A few examples are the adoption of the European Convention on Spectator Violence and Misbehaviour at Sports Events and in particular Football Matches, European Commission 1 Dec. 1999, The Helsinki report, COM (1999) 644, 6, and the ratification of the narcotics charter in 1994.

8. In the Netherlands, non-commercial sports clubs are the most important framework for organized sports activities, even more so than schools. They are usually affiliated with the national sports federation for their branch of sports. These clubs historically came from the 'pillarization' and were culturally defined. Nowadays, this strict denominational segregation no longer plays an important role. These sports clubs can be organized in different ways and it is important to take a closer look at these different variations. Due to the increasing professionality of sports clubs they can earn profits up to millions of euros and at that level the legal entity is a key element of the club, especially in the soccer industry. In 2002 it became possible for commercial companies to become a member of the KNVB and to get a licence to join the competition, which was a need that had existed for a long time. It is also proof of the professionalization of sports in the Netherlands. The sportive task and the commercial goal are inseparably connected to one another and since sports organizations have started to develop more and more into actual commercial companies instead of non-profit organizations, the legal form chosen is important.

9. All these different legal entities have in common that they are incorporated, which means that the management has the obligation to fulfil its task in the best interests of the entity, according to Article 2:9 Dutch Civil Code (BW) but is (in general) not liable for any claims towards the company. In this respect, there is no substantial difference among these business entities. However, in case of supervision of the management board, there is a difference, which will be discussed in the following paragraphs. The main difference between an incorporated company and an association is that one can become a member of association and not of an incorporated company. An incorporated company is owned by the shareholders. These shares are transmissible. This creates the possibility of a change of control, which ought not to change the business internally, but in reality, another person (or organization) comes into control. The effects of this should not be underestimated.

§2. Foundation (*Stichting*)

10. A foundation is a not-for-profit organization, which can be founded by a single person. In case of a sports foundation, gaining profits is only a means to achieve the main goal, explicitly mentioned in the statutes and by-laws, which is to practice sports on a certain level. This goal is usually not commercial and has to be achieved with the help of a certain amount of (minimum) capital. The by-laws confirm the not-for-profit character of the legal entity. Notwithstanding this, a foundation can spend its profits if this is in accordance with the goal set forth in the by-laws and the idealistic or social perspective expressed in Article 2:285 lid 3 BW. In any other case it is prohibited. Acting contradictory to the by-laws requires either an amendment of that specific provision or a legal transition into an association. It is possible to instate a supervisory board within the foundation. Members of a supervisory board tend to possess qualities and knowledge, which will, in the long term, improve the management, because they will provide adequate supervision. A foundation cannot have members, which is the main difference from an association.

11. On 1 July 2021 a new act came into force on the oversight of associations and foundations. It is called: The Act Governance and Oversight on legal entities (WBTR). The goal of this new legislation is to align the rules on oversight in associations and foundations with those of (commercial) legal entities like the Company with Limited Liability (BV) and the Company Limited by Shares (NV). From 1 July 2021 the possibility to instate a Board of Commissioners is now enshrined in the law. There is however an obligation to instate such a board. This also applies to the possibility of instating a one-tier board (review paragraph 15 concerning the subject of the one-tier board below); there always was a possibility to instate a one-tier board in a foundation or associations, but this will have a legal basis as well because of the WBTR.

A new consideration for the board of associations and foundation is the explicit task to always act in the best interests of the association or foundation, which at this moment is only part of the regulations concerning NV's and BV's. Furthermore, if a conflict of interest arises for one of the board members, he may no longer participate in the decision-making on this subject. Some by-laws of sports associations (i.e., the model for by-laws provided by de KNVB) already have such a provision. Next to this the by-laws of associations must contain a provision of the case that all the board members are incapacitated (i.e., when they are ill or have been suspended or fired). Associations are obliged to instate such a provision when they decide to first change their by-laws after the entry into force of the WBTR (so there is no immediate need to change the by-laws on 1 July 2021).

In regard to voting of a board member during decision-making, one board member may no longer have more votes than all the other board members combined. This is to prevent one board member from obtaining all the power in the board. In case such a provision was made in the current by-laws, they are automatically annihilated five years from the entry into force of the WBTR.

Another important change because of the Wet Toezicht en Bestuur Rechtspersonen/ Act on Oversight en Governance of legal Entities (WTBR) is the liability of board members in case of bankruptcy of the association. If the board seriously neglects its tasks and this is the probable cause of the bankruptcy, the board members might be liable for the deficit of claims that cannot be paid.

§3. Association (*Vereniging*)

12. An association is a not-for-profit organization, which can be founded by at least two or more members. This implies that the articles of association have to be established jointly as well. Proof that these members act together in one way or another exists is sufficient to establish an association. In that case the association is not considered to be a legal entity. To attain the status of a legal entity the association has to be registered at the chamber of commerce. In case of a sports association, gaining profits is only a means to achieve the main non-commercial goal, which is to practice sports on a certain level. Any gain cannot be divided among the members;[16] an association is an altruistic organization. It follows that any profits cannot be divided among the management board either. This does not mean that members of the management board are not allowed to receive remuneration for their services. The annual meeting of members is similar to the annual meeting of shareholders in the companies with limited liability or limited by shares. They have some binding enforceable obligations, such as, to determine the annual account and to control, approve or dismiss the management board. The members who are involved in the organization of the association are obliged to realize the common goals in the best interest of the association. For shareholders this is slightly different, since they may pursue their own best interests and gain an optimal return on their investment. Providing an advisory board (RvC) is not a common policy in associations but is highly recommended since an advisory board is a more effective tool for supervision.

§4. Company with Limited Liability and the Company Limited by Shares

13. These types of companies are tailored for the development of commercial activities and gaining profits. Therefore, it is usually easier for this legal entity to attract capital. In a company with limited liability and a company limited by shares, profits may be issued towards its shareholders, since it is the goal of these types of entities to be profitable organizations; this is no different with respect to sports. It is preferable to choose these types of corporations, since they provide a 'wonder formula' for a better image and business-like character; it provides the possibility to attract foreign capital. The articles of association can expand or restrict co-determination. Setting up a group structure[17] further professionalizes sports activities and provides a limitation in responsibilities for members of the board. The annual meeting of shareholders and the RvC are the instruments to control the management of the company. It is the supervisory board's task to supervise the board's policy-making and day-to-day business management[18] in the best interest of the company,[19] while the management of the company has to consult the annual meeting of shareholders every year. Shareholders are usually more interested in their own best interest, which is to gain as much profit as possible from their investment. With this goal comes the possibility to transfer shares, resulting in a possible change of control, which can have a crucial influence on a sports organization. The NV is the only form which can attract money by doing an initial public offering (IPO) or issuing stocks on a stock exchange. In the Netherlands only one sports club is listed at the Amsterdam Stock Exchange (AEX), which is the Amsterdam football club Ajax. Europe-wide twenty-two football clubs are listed at a stock exchange. The BV

16. Article 2:26 lid 3 BW.
17. Example, the PSV Eindhoven structure.
18. *See* Arts 2:140 and 2:250 BW.
19. *See* Arts 2:142 and 2:252, Arts 2:158 and 2:268, 2:162a and 2:271a BW, dealing with the so-called structuurregime.

and the NV also have some tax advantages and it can be profitable to set up a secondary group structure, which can be organized for more profits. This can create blurred group structures, which in general is not desirable. However, it is a fact that in the choice of a legal structure, tax and financial consequences play a key role. However, as mentioned above, the choice can also be influenced by the fact that these legal entities have a more professional image, which can benefit the company.

14. The bill on management and supervision has led to changes in company law with regard to managing and supervisory directors of legal entities. The majority of provisions apply to both NVs and BVs. The most sweeping changes also apply to foundations. A few provisions only relate to listed companies. The legislation came into force on 1 January 2013.[20]

One-Tier Board (NV and BV)

15. A statutory basis is introduced for the creation of a one-tier board. Companies including those governed by the 'structure regime' – will be able to choose between a one-tier or two-tier board. Traditionally, management of Dutch companies has been based on a two-tier system, with a managing board and a separate supervisory board. The new one-tier board consists of both executive and non-executive directors. To create a one-tier board, the by-laws must be amended to provide that the management tasks are divided among one or more executive directors and one or more non-executive directors. The choice between a one-tier board and a two-tier board does make a significant material difference in practice.

Restrictions on Number of Supervisory Positions (Large NV, BV and Foundation)

Provisions have been introduced in 2013 limiting the number of supervisory positions that managing and supervisory directors of certain entities may hold.[21]

Restrictions

16. If a legal entity meets the criteria set out below, the appointment of executive or non-executive directors, managing directors, supervisory directors or members of a supervisory body is subject to the following restrictions:

- A person may only be appointed as a *managing/executive director* if he/she holds *no more than two supervisory positions* at other entities which are governed by the same restrictions and does not hold the position of chairman of the supervisory board or one-tier board at such other entity.
- A person may only be appointed as *supervisory director, non-executive director or member of a supervisory body* if he/she holds *no more than four supervisory positions* at other entities which are governed by the same restrictions. In this connection, the position of chairman equals two positions.

20. Amending the Civil Code Book 2 (amendment rules on management and control in public and private companies).
21. *See* Arts 2:132a and 2:242a BW.

- The term *supervisory position* means the position of supervisory director, non-executive director or member of a supervisory board that has been set up pursuant to the articles of association.
- Supervisory positions at several entities belonging to the same group constitute one position.
- Supervisory positions *at foreign entities* are *not* taken into account.
- An appointment by the Enterprise Chamber (Ondernemingskamer) as part of corporate inquiry proceedings is *not* taken into account.

Criteria for Applicability of Restrictions

17. The restrictions concerning the number of supervisory positions held apply to NVs, BVs and foundations which qualify as 'large' entities *and* meet the 'entry transition' criteria.

What Is a 'Large' Entity?

18. An NV, BV or foundation qualifies as a 'large' entity if at least *two* of the following three criteria are met:[22]

(1) The value of the assets according to the balance sheet with explanatory notes exceeds EUR 20 million.
(2) The net turnover for the financial year exceeds EUR 40 million.
(3) There are, on average, two-hundred and fifty or more employees during the fiscal year.

Date of reference for qualifying as 'large' is the date of the balance sheet. If there are consolidated accounts, these will be used as a basis.

Entry and Exit Transition

19. The restrictions on the number of supervisory positions apply when an NV, BV or foundation qualifies as 'large' on two consecutive balance sheet dates *('entry transition')*. Thus, if an entity's fiscal year is the same as the calendar year and the entity qualifies as 'large' on 31 December 2019 and on 31 December 2020, the restrictions apply from 31 December 2020.

If an NV, BV or foundation no longer qualifies as large on two consecutive balance sheet dates, the restrictions on the number of supervisory positions cease to apply ('exit transition').

22. *See* Art. 2:397 para. 1.

Which Large Foundations?

20. The restrictions on the number of supervisory positions only apply to a large foundation if it has a statutory obligation to draw up annual accounts or a similar document. Large charitable, cultural, academic and religious foundations do not have to comply with the restrictions provided that they do not engage in commercial activities and do not have to draft financial statements. Large non-profit organizations such as care providers and housing organizations are subject to these restrictions because specific legislation requires them to draft financial statements. If a foundation voluntarily drafts these as part of an application for a subsidy, this does not cause the restrictions to apply, according to the Minister.

Appointment Null and Void

21. If an appointment causes a managing/executive director or a supervisory/non-executive director to hold more than the maximum number of supervisory positions, that appointment is null and void. This, however, does *not* affect the validity of decisions taken by the director in question.[23]

Conflict of Interest

(NV/BV)

22. If an executive/managing director has a conflict of interest, he/she may not *participate in the discussion and decision-making* of the board about the conflicted subject.[24] These rules also apply to conflicted supervisory/non-executive directors. If the director breaches this rule, the decision can be nullified. These new statutory provisions are of a mandatory nature and may not be deviated from.

23. Under the law, the relationship between a managing/executive director and a listed company cannot be treated as an employment contract. But the law does not specify the nature of the relationship. In practice, it will be treated as a mandate agreement (*'overeenkomst van opdracht'*). Directors of non-listed companies can have a labour agreement or both a labour agreement and a managing agreement.

§5. Implications in the Future

24. The fact that top sports have become a billion-euro industry as they become more and more professionalized cannot be denied. The availability of the possibility to set up new business forms in the sports industry can be a new impulse for the development of top sports. That possibility alone can provide a valid argument for the acceptance of for-profit business forms next to not-for-profit business forms. However, it has to be kept in mind that shares are transmissible and, therefore, all control can be transferred into one set of hands. This single shareholder may not act in the best interests of the company, but rather in his own best interests to gain as

23. *See* Arts 2:132a/242a para. 3 BW.
24. *See* Arts 2:129/20239 para. 6 BW.

much profit as possible from his investment. This possible consequence could become a threat to the fairness of a sports competition as determined by the rules of fair competition in sports. Therefore, further strengthening of rules regulating fairness in sports is required.

25. With respect to the national organization of sports it is important that every club, no matter what entity has been chosen, abides by rules and decisions of the sports federation in order to ensure fair competition. This implies that every member of the club should also be a member of the federation, because the federation can then exercise control over all the clubs. With respect to the club management and the supervisory board these rules can apply as well to make sure that they will adapt to the provisions of the federation and will not be able to escape the disciplinary regime. Any legal form of doing business can then be adapted to the wishes of each federation. However, the fact that shareholders are involved, and the fact that shares are transmissible, becomes a complicating factor. From a legal point of view, it is possible to combine the fact that someone is a shareholder in a sports club with membership in a sports federation, for example, by adding a provision to that effect in the by-laws. This will only work if the shares are registered by name; then the shares cannot be assigned to a non-member of the federation and termination of membership in the federation can be combined with an obligation to transfer back the shares. Non-compliance with these provisions could be punishable by disqualification from the competition. What also deserves some extra attention is the role of a single shareholder who has no (sportive) interest in the club, but whose personal financial interest could lead to a serious distortion of competition. In theory, the situation could arise where one shareholder owns multiple clubs in the same sport. This shareholder can have an undue influence in this competition that can lead to falsification of competition. Only the by-laws can provide a solution to this situation by, for example, establishing an exclusivity shareholder clause or a limitation on the influence of the sole shareholder on the management and supervisory board. In 2002, the KNVB chose clear membership requirements within a flexible system with a large amount of freedom to provide optimal organization for the business. This translates into limiting the possible influence of the single shareholder. The KNVB membership rules require an independent organ to determine the influence of shareholders in the annual meeting and the composition of both management and supervisory boards, approval of important decisions, etc. This organ is the meeting of shareholders with priority shareholders. Furthermore, the KNVB closely looks at the percentage of club shareholders who are not members of the federation and, therefore, can be considered less than reliable. Since the KNVB has not chosen a system which combines shareholdership with membership, this needs to be closely monitored. The KNVB has drafted the 'Guidelines to safeguard independence and continuity licence holders' which state rules as to what kind of safeguards the by-laws of the clubs must contain in regard to change of control due to transfer of shares. The goal of these guidelines is to protect the independence of the organizations towards the shareholders. It is also important to avoid a possible conflict of interest. This has to be dealt with in the articles of association by a statutory incompatibility: a member of the management board cannot be a member of the supervisory board and vice versa. This rule should also be adapted to shareholders. If, in any event, a situation occurs which is contradictory to the above-mentioned provisions, the shareholder should be prohibited from practising his legal rights and should be obliged to offer his shares to the market. This obligatory announcement of an illegal situation provides the KNVB with sufficient tools to control and adjust unfair situations. In the end, the social and competitive aspect of sports should be safeguarded, even if (or perhaps because) huge amounts of money are involved.

Part II. Sports and Status

Chapter 1. General Issues

§1. Labour Law in Relation to Sports

26. In the Netherlands, there are no specific general statutory regulations or laws regarding the legal status of professional sportsmen. However, the sportsman is mentioned separately in several acts, especially in social security acts. This means that 'general' labour law regulates the legal status of sportsmen. Besides general labour law, one should bear in mind the internal regulations of the sports club and the sports associations of which the sportsman or woman is a member.

27. Dutch labour law is not laid down in one particular act. The contractual relationship between employer and employee is mainly regulated by the BW. In Book 7 of the BW, Title 10 is entirely devoted to the employment contract.[25] Since the tenth title is a part of the BW, the general provisions with respect to the law of obligations generally apply to the law of employment contracts. Because of the so-called layered structure of the Dutch BW, general law only applies in case the specific laws do not regulate a subject. Collective labour law can be considered part of the law of obligations as well. However, collective labour law is specified by a number of particular legal provisions. We will return to this subject below. It is important to note that it is possible to deviate from some of these obligations. This possibility is included in the specific articles and might stipulate conditions for deviation. Some of these articles can only be deviated from by means of a CLA.

§2. Labour Relations in General and in Sports in Particular

28. In the Netherlands, trade unions arose in the early 1900s. As a result of this, nowadays there are a number of different central trade unions. Major central trade unions are the National Federation of Trade Unions/*Federatie Nederlandse Vakbeweging* (FNV) and the National Federation of Christian Trade Unions/*Christelijke Nederlandse Vakbeweging* (CNV). A large number of sectoral trade unions are affiliated to these central trade unions. These trade unions focus on one or several specific branches of the economy. Besides these two unions, there are a number of non-affiliated trade unions. There are also many employer's associations. On a

25. Articles 7:610–7:691 of the Civil Code deal with this subject.

national level, these employer's associations are usually affiliated with a larger national association: VNO–NCW (large companies), MKB–Nederland (small- and medium-sized businesses) and LTO Nederland (agricultural industry).

§3. The Collective Labour Agreement

29. The CLA is a written contract between a trade union and an employer or an employer's association regarding the terms of employment within (a section of) the employment organization (or its members). In the Netherlands, the contracting trade unions do not have to meet particular requirements, provided that the trade union is a registered association with statutory competence to enter into CLAs. Likewise, Dutch legislation does not include requirements of representativeness for trade unions to enforce admittance to collective bargaining. In the worst case, trade unions have to enforce access to collective bargaining by means of strikes; in addition to strikes it is possible to organize slow-downs and punctuality actions. The employer has a free choice of entering into a CLA with a trade union as desired. For the sake of completeness, attention should be drawn to the fact that a CLA has no effect until it is registered at the office of the Minister of Social Affairs and Employment (SZW) and a confirmation has been received.[26] This does not mean that a quality check regarding the content takes place, and the registration is a mere instrument to monitor the number of CLAs in effect and their content. A CLA is registered by sending it to the Ministry of Social Affairs and Employment. In practice, registration is never a problem, since the commencement of the agreement can take place after registration with retroactive effect.

30. What is agreed upon by the CLA is binding for the parties involved. The case law on CLAs shows that members of the trade unions and/or the members of the employer's associations involved are bound by the collective agreement.[27] The CLA's stipulations are a part of the individual employment contract, in so far as these stipulations are intended to have a continued effect on individual employment contracts. Next to this it is possible for the trade unions to agree on binding stipulations with the employer themselves, specifically to govern their relationship. In this respect the so-called peace clauses and agreements on facilitated trade union activities in the company should be considered.

31. The CLA does not directly bind non-members of trade unions. However, Article 14 Collective Labour Agreement Act (WCAO) states that the employer is obliged to apply the CLAs to this group of employees (so-called Article 14-employees) as well. This should prevent unequal treatment and restrain employers from hiring only non-members. These non-members however cannot enforce compliance with the CLA's stipulations in a court of law. The CLA can only be enforced when a provision concerning the non-member's individual employment contract declares the CLA applicable.

---

26. Article 4 Wlv.
27. Article 9, WCAO.

32. In accordance with the Act on the Declaration of the Universally Binding and Non-binding Status of Collective Labour Agreements (WAVV), it is possible to declare a CLA binding for all employers and employees in a specific branch of trade. This results in the CLA acquiring the status of law. Because of this, even non-members of a trade union employed by non-bound employers can derive rights from that CLA. To achieve this result the Minister of Social Affairs and Employment must decide that the CLA is binding upon all employers and employees in the specific branch of a trade. The declaration is generally binding for a period of two years at the most. It is only possible to declare a CLA binding on all employers and employees in the specific branch of a trade when the stipulations of that CLA apply to the majority of employees in a certain branch in a part of the nation or nationwide. It is a common practice for CLAs to be declared binding on all employers and employees in the specific branch of a trade.

33. In practice, the question regularly arises what the legal status of the CLA's stipulations is, after the expiration date of the CLA or the end of the generally binding period. The Dutch Supreme Court (HR) has decided repeatedly that when a CLA expires, its stipulations continue to have effect. This means that these stipulations will remain in force until a new CLA has come into effect. In the case of the expiry of a CLA which has been declared generally binding (AVV), the Supreme Court has decided that the need to observe these stipulations ends immediately. Currently, important CLAs with respect to sports include:[28]

- Sports CLAs (applying to employees in the service of important sporting organizations (including KNVB and NOC*NSF) as well as provincial sporting organizations).
- CLAs for multifunctional sports and fitness centres.
- CLAs for professional football players in the Netherlands (there are a couple of separate CLAs for female football players).
- CLAs for trainer/manager in professional football.
- CLA for professional cyclists.
- CLA for sport associations.
- CLA for professional ice hockey players, Tilburg Trappers.

34. In the past, the question has presented itself how to assess the terms of a CLA. Should one consider the purpose of the parties involved, for example? The HR has answered this question. According to the Supreme Court, one should interpret the terms literally, considering the context of the complete text.[29] Similar phrasing used elsewhere in the CLA and the legal consequences which the various textual interpretations provide should therefore be taken into account as well. Next to this, officially written explanatory texts may be used in the interpretation.[30] No other

28. For more on this subject: S.F.H. Jellinghaus (ed.) *Capta Sportrecht*, Antwerpen/s'-Hertogenbosch 2021: Gompel & Scavina, pp. 161–165 and S.F.H. Jellinghaus and P. van Minnen Arbeidsrecht/ WWZ en de CAO in: Sport en Recht, editie 23, Nieuwegein 2019.
29. For example, HR 17 Sep. 1993, NJ 1994, 173 and HR 24 Sep. 1993, JAR 1993/236.
30. HR 4 May 2018, ECLI:NL:HR:2018:678.

information than the above mentioned may be used to interpret the text of the CLA. The rationale behind this is the fact that the employee has not been directly involved in the collective bargaining; because of this the employee has not gained a clear insight into the background (including the purposes of the parties involved) of the agreement. This means that the phrasing of the CLA text is extremely important.

§4. The Works Council

35. On the basis of the Works Councils Act (WOR), every employer who employs more than fifty employees is obliged to set up a works council.[31] The works council is instated for the benefit of the company's effective functioning and consists only of employees, who are elected by the employees of the company. The works council has a number of statutory rights at its disposal, namely:

(1) the right to deliberation;[32]
(2) the right to information;[33]
(3) the power of initiative;[34]
(4) advisory powers;[35]
(5) the power of approval.[36]

These rights can be extended by means of a written agreement, for example, a CLA.

36. The first two rights result in the circumstance that the works council is entitled to consult with and ask questions to the executive (the so-called *bestuurder*) responsible for the execution of labour within the company; the director or manager. The works council can make suggestions to which the employer is obliged to react. The works council's most important rights are the right to prior consultation and the power of approval or consent.

37. Without previously obtaining the works council's advice, the employer is not allowed to take those decisions that are stated in the WOR.[37] The application for advice and the description of an intended decision should give insight into the grounds for the decision and the expected consequences for employees as well as the way in which these negative consequences are to be avoided. The advisory powers concern the following intended decisions:

31. Article 2, WOR. If desired, works councils can be set up on a voluntary basis, for example, on the basis of a CLA, where there are fewer than fifty employees.
32. Article 23, WOR.
33. Articles 31 et seq., WOR.
34. Article 23, s. 3, WOR.
35. Article 25, WOR.
36. Article 27, WOR.
37. Article 25, s. 1, WOR. If desired, these rights can be extended in writing on a voluntary basis Art. 32, WOR.

- transfer of control of the company or of a division of the company;
- the establishment, the taking over or the entering into an association to take control over another company, as well as concluding an alliance with, substantially altering or breaking off a long-lasting cooperation with another company, including entering into, substantially altering or breaking off a substantial financial participation due to or for the benefit of such a company;
- the termination of the company's activities or a substantial part of these activities;
- a substantial reduction, extension or other alteration in the activities of the company;
- a substantial alteration in the organization of the company, or in the distribution of the powers within the organization;
- changing the location from which the company performs its activities;
- recruiting or hiring workers group wise;
- making a substantial investment for the benefit of the company;
- attracting substantial credit for the benefit of the company;
- extending a substantial credit and providing collateral for substantial debts of another company, unless it occurs in the normal conduct of the activities of business;
- introducing or altering important technological facilities;
- taking important measures in connection with the company's concern for the environment, including making arrangements or altering policy, organizational and administrative facilities regarding the environment;
- applying for an exemption with regard to bearing the risk, as mentioned in Article 40, section 1, Wet financiering sociale verzekeringen/Act on Financing Social Security;
- referring and formulating an advisory task to an expert from outside the company regarding one of the above-mentioned matters;
- the nomination or dismissal of executives.

38. If the employer fails to comply with the works council's advisory rights, the works council may enforce its right by legal measures or proceedings. The employer is obliged to respond in writing with respect to the works councils advice. If the employer does not follow the works councils advice he must explain his reasons to do so. Subsequently, the works council has the possibility of taking the matter to court where a judge will examine the employer's decision. The court will have to decide whether the decision is (evidently) unreasonable. A separate right to prior consultation refers to the works council's right to advise in matters concerning the dismissal or the appointment of the director or executive of the company and the above-mentioned executive of the works council.[38] Contrary to the right to prior consultation discussed above, the works council cannot go to court in case the advice of the works council is not followed.

39. In respect to the establishment, alteration or withdrawal of a number of explicitly mentioned regulations concerning employment conditions, the works

38. Article 30, WOR.

council has the power of approval.[39] This means that these decisions cannot be taken without the previously obtained consent of the works council. This right of approval affects regulations concerning:

- pension, profit-sharing regulations or savings regulations;
- working hours or holiday regulations;
- remuneration or job evaluation systems;
- the field of working conditions or the absence because of illness;
- the field of appointment, dismissal or promotion policy;
- the field of employee education;
- the field of employee evaluation;
- the field of company welfare work;
- the field of discussion of progress of work;
- the field of consideration of complaints;
- the registration, handling and protection of personal data of the employees in the company;
- the provisions aimed at or suitable for observation or checks on the presence, behaviour or performance of employees in the company;
- a procedure on how to handle the report of a suspected irregularity, Article 2, section 1, Wet Huis voor Klokkenluiders (Whistle-blowers act).

40. This power of approval is not applicable when a CLA provides a regulation for the matter concerned. When the works council does not give its approval, the employer has to take the matter to court in order to request the approval of the court as a substitute for the approval of the works council. This request will only be granted when the refusal to approve is unreasonable or when the decision is required for substantial business organizational reasons, business social reasons or reasons of business economics.

41. In addition, attention should be drawn to the fact that members of the works council have the right to receive education and have the right to facilities at the employer's expense, including meeting during working hours. Works councils regularly bargain about the terms of employment, too. However, there is no legal basis for this. Furthermore, employment law offers the (candidate) members of the works council legal protection. Members of the works council retain their right to remuneration during the time they work for the works council.

42. For the sake of completeness, it should be pointed out that there is a particular regulation with respect to companies with at least ten employees and fewer than fifty employees. These companies are not obliged to instate a works council. However, it is possible to set up a committee of staff representatives. When the majority of the personnel requests it, the employer is obliged to set up such representatives. This committee consists of at least three people who are elected by all employees by means of an election with anonymous ballots. The staff representatives have the right to consult with their employer and the right to ask questions which must be

39. Article 27, WOR.

answered. Furthermore, the employee representatives have the power of approval with respect to the establishment, alteration or withdrawal of working hours regulations and regulations in the field of working conditions, absence through illness or reintegration policy.

43. When staff representatives have not been set up, an employer who employs at least ten employees and fewer than fifty employees is in any case obliged to arrange a collective meeting with all employees twice a year. This meeting has to take place if at least one-fourth of all employees request it. During this meeting all relevant matters can be discussed. Moreover, employees must have the opportunity to advise on intended employer decisions that may lead to possible job losses.

44. In sports, alternative employee participation often takes place. First of all, sportsmen have the right of consultation regarding their membership in national sporting associations. A system of employee participation is regularly created through internal regulations of sporting associations on behalf of (professional) sportsmen. Likewise, the KNVB regulations provide for a Central Players Council (CSR), which looks after the interests of professional football players. The CSR has the following rights:

(1) advisory powers with regard to particular matters, including the decree of KNVB regulations;
(2) the right to challenge the appointment of KNVB committee members and KNVB members of the board;
(3) the power of approval with respect to, for example, a reorganization of the KNVB.

Chapter 2. Public Regulation

§1. Qualification of Legal Status

I. Amateur

45. Dutch law makes no distinction between the concept of amateur or professional sportsmen. Whether a person is an amateur or professional sportsperson should be decided in the light of all the facts and circumstances and this will determine whether social security contributions and taxes are to be paid. Nevertheless, in the legal literature a distinction has been made between amateurs and professionals. Some authors assume that the distinction between professional and amateur sports is not a result of the institutionalization of the sportsmen but a result of the organization of the sports involved.[40] In any case, many segments of sports have particular stipulations with respect to the question of whether people are amateur or professional sportsmen (with regard to football, *see*, for example, the regulations *Amateurbepalingen*); therefore, to some extent sports associations can define the legal status of their athletes.

46. In addition, NOC*NSF acknowledges the distinction between top-class sport statuses at A-level, B-level or HP-level (high-potential). This concerns sportsmen who are competing at international level (European championships, world championships and the Olympics) within a generally recognized sports discipline. These sportsmen receive a subsidy by which they are able to support themselves so that they can fully focus on practising top-class sports. Within the sphere of social security, a special position is created for the benefit of these sportsmen to assure them of employee insurance, including insurance for medical expenses and disability. In addition, there are particular sponsorship facilities for the benefit of these sportsmen. The national organization of sporting associations, NOC*NSF, takes responsibility for these facilities.

II. Self-Employment

47. Instead of offering the intended employee an employment contract, athletes are sometimes allowed to practice as self-employed workers. In most cases the person in question will be able to make more money that way, and the employer is not bound by labour law provisions. Dutch labour law (and dismissal law in particular) is sometimes regarded as rigid and not fitting to the special position of athletes. As this is the case, it is possible to perform activities as a self-employed person. In that case, it is necessary for the person in question to work as a self-employed person in practice; in particular, the person in question needs to be able to perform his activities by his own free will (obviously within the general legal framework). Moreover, Dutch law assumes the existence of an employment contract if someone works

40. H.T. van Staveren & M.J.G. Das, Knelpunten in de rechtspositie van de topsporter [Sticking points in the legal position of professional sportsmen], VU 1990.

weekly for payment for at least three months or at least twenty hours a month for at least three months. This means that the burden of proof with respect to the existence of an employment contract is reversed. The employer has to prove that the employment contract does not exist.

48. Under social security legislation and tax legislation, it is important to define whether someone is working as an employee, or whether a person runs an enterprise. Moreover, the earning of 'wages' is broadly interpreted. In several benefit agencies' directives, indications are included of what matters will be considered relevant in defining wages.[41] In that regard the following matters are significant, but not decisive:

– registration with the Chamber of Commerce;
– having one's own office space at one's disposal;
– canvassing (e.g., advertising and sponsoring);
– independent operational management;
– working with a checked model agreement by Dutch Tax authorities.

49. Having several clients is considered very important in establishing the existence of an enterprise. Possibly these standards are applied less strictly during the initial phase. The question of whether the self-employed person has the freedom to conduct his activities in accordance with his own views is very important in this matter (the absence of a relationship of authority) as well.

As of 1 May 2016, the self-employed person and the employer/principal can use a model agreement checked by Dutch Tax authorities to have more certainty in advance about the employment relationship.

The goal of this legislation was for employers/principals to gain the certainty that they did not have to pay taxes as an employer. The provisions are contained in the Act on Deregulation Qualification of Labour Relations (DBA). In cooperation with industries and profession interest groups, the Dutch Tax Authorities drew up a system of model agreements for employers/principals or their intermediaries and individual contractors.

The model contracts are available on Belastingdienst.nl. If employers/principals and self-employed work in accordance with the model agreements, they would have the required assurance about the income tax in advance for a period of five years. Practice has proved that this law did not provide the expected clarity to parties. The government has thus decided to replace the Act Deregulating labour relations with new legislation. This new legislation will contain minimum wages for self-employed workers. In short, a person is expected to be an actually independent self-employed worker if he earns at least EUR 16 per hour. In case the worker has to make more hours than expected, the client has to make sure the fee per hour will not drop below EUR 16. If a worker earns at least EUR 75 per hour he can obtain a guaranty that his client does not have to pay taxes for employers. This new law is

41. In particular, *see* the guidance assessment agreements labour relations [Handreiking beoordelingskader overeenkomsten arbeidsrelaties (Handreiking DBA)] www.belastingdienst.nl.

expected to be in force somewhere during 2021. Until then the tax authorities will not actively check if a self-employed worker is actually an employee.

50. This issue also arises when volunteers are enlisted and whether these people are receiving financial compensation for expenses in return. A small compensation is allowed by the tax authorities. The volunteer may receive a fee of up to EUR 5 per hour with a maximum of EUR 180 per month and in total EUR 1,800 per year in 2021. These limits apply to the total sum that can be given as compensation for the deployment. In this case, too, it should be considered in the light of the relevant facts and circumstances whether it is a matter of a (fictitious) employment contract. In this connection, the Central Appeals Tribunal judged that a gymnastic club, which was managed by volunteers, was free to supply its gymnastic leaders with a payment for expenses to the extent of EUR 2–8 per hour. The Central Appeals Tribunal considered that this form of cooperation left no room for a relationship of authority within the meaning of labour law.[42] On the other hand, the Tribunal judged that in the case of a head coach in cricket there was a relationship of authority. This relationship was deduced from the head coach's obligations, including an obligation to appear on demand.[43]

III. Employment Contract

A. Commencement of Employment

51. The fact is that an employment contract forms a part of general Dutch civil law. Basically, this means that the usual requirements of contracts are applicable, namely they will enter into the contract and the acceptance of an offer. Recently the HR ruled that it is no longer relevant whether parties involved wanted to enter into an employment contract or not.[44] The qualification of the contract should be done on the basis of objective legal criteria.

52. The fact that a contract can be considered to be an employment contract results in the applicability of the safeguards of employment law. The relationship has to meet the following requirements during a certain time:[45]

(1) to earn wages;
(2) to perform labour; and
(3) to accept the existence of a relationship of authority.

These aspects are relevant, in particular, since there are no formal requirements regarding the establishment of an employment contract, such as that it has to be in

42. CRvB, 4 Sep. 1997, USZ 1997/249.
43. CRvB, 4 Dec. 1997, USZ 1998/39.
44. HR 6 Nov. 2020, ECLI:NL:HR:2020:1746.
45. Article 7:610 Civil Code.

writing. If one of the above-mentioned factors does not exist in the relationship, it cannot have the status of employment contract.

A CLA as discussed above can only be applicable to an employment contract. Because of this many CLAs instruct the organization which is bound by its rules to enter into employment contracts with athletes. This goes the same for some of the by-laws of large federations such as the KNVB.

53. The concept of 'earning wages' implies that employees receive some fee for their activities. In an employment contract, the law provides further requirements, among which is the level of wages. This will be discussed below. The requirement 'to perform labour' means that the employee performs labour on behalf of the employer. These activities should be performed by the person himself.[46] Therefore, the employee is not allowed to have his activities performed by another person as a substitute. The requirement of a 'relationship of authority' means that the employee is subordinate to the employer and, therefore, has to carry out instructions within reasonable limits.[47] Whether these requirements are met has to be examined in the light of the factual situation;[48] the content of a written agreement is not decisive. Therefore, it is not possible to evade the safeguards pertaining to employment law by agreeing otherwise in writing. In practice mainly the question of whether or not a relationship of authority exists causes for debate. The other two criteria are usually easy to determine, but the criterium of having a relationship of authority has to be filled in with factual information and is often debatable. This is especially the case in our changing society where people are more and more independent and free in the way they carry out their tasks.

54. In response to a proliferation of flexible working relationships, the Dutch legislator has made it easier for an employee to prove the actual existence of an employment contract. For that reason, the law prescribes that when a person performs labour for payment during a period of three consecutive months, weekly or for twenty hours a month, that person is presumed to perform these activities under an employment contract. Because of this, the burden of proof regarding the existence of an employment contract is shifted to the employer, who must prove that the parties did not enter into an employment contract.[49]

55. Especially in sports, extensive negotiations usually take place before the commencement of employment. Negotiating parties are not free to unexpectedly

46. Article 7:659 Civil Code.
47. Article 7:660 Civil Code.
48. For example, Arbitration Tribunal KNVB, 30 Jan. 2002, No. 886, Sportzaken 2002/1, No. 21, B1 *Ten Bhömer v. Duno and Arbitration Tribunal KNVB*, 8 Oct. 2001, No. 862, Sportzaken 2001/4 (No. 20) B2, A2/Connoly, Court of Appeal Leeuwarden, 12 Feb. 2003, Sportzaken 2002/4 (No. 24) B7 Timmer/de Vegt), Arbitration Tribunal KNVB, 9 Jan. 2013, nr. 1358, Central counsel of appeal, 4 Sep. 2013, ECLI:NL:CRVB:2013:BZ6883.
49. Article 7:610A Civil Code.

and suddenly end these negotiations. According to Dutch case law (NJ), the process of negotiation can be divided into three phases:[50]

- Phase 1: Each party is free to withdraw from negotiations.
- Phase 2: A party is no longer free simply to break off negotiations. When a party in this phase breaks off negotiations, it can be held liable for damages.
- Phase 3: Negotiations have progressed to the point where breaking off will put the withdrawing party under the obligation to pay damages to the other party involved.

For the sake of completeness, we note that there is discussion among scholars as to whether the Supreme Court still upholds three phases or, after a verdict in 2005,[51] recognizes only two phases and the second phase is no longer in play.

56. CLAs and the internal regulations of sporting associations often prescribe that employment contracts are to be entered into in writing.[52] Such a regulation does not alter what has been stated above; when there is no written employment contract, there can still be a legally valid employment contract. In that case, the above-mentioned presumptions of law apply. For the sake of completeness, it should be mentioned that the coordinating sporting association frequently demands a working relationship between a club and its sportsmen. In that case, the independent entrepreneurship of the sportsmen will not be tolerated. The Dutch cycling association is an example of this. This association only issues a permit in case of a working relationship between the club and the sportsman. A similar requirement applies to professional football players.

57. In sports, it is a normal phenomenon to pay the sportsman an agreed amount of money at the commencement of employment (signing bonus). According to case law of the Arbitration Tribunal KNVB and the judges of the court, whether this money should be considered wages according to civil law should be tested by considering all relevant facts and circumstances.[53] The effect of this payment could be construed as an employment relationship.

B. The Contents of the Employment Contract

58. The principle of the parties being free to determine the contents of the employment contract also applies in the Netherlands. However, the law prescribes

50. HR 18 Jun. 1982, NJ 1983, 723 Plas/Valburg and HR 23 Oct. 1987, NJ 1988, 1017 and HR 31 May 1991, NJ 1991, 647 Skil/wielerploeg Vogelaar. For example, *see* Arbitration Tribunal KNVB, No. 786, Sportzaken 2000/3 (No. 15) B1 Go Ahead Eagles/Zonneveld and NEC and President of the court, Leeuwarden, 6 Apr. 2001, Sportzaken 2001/4 (No. 20) B5 Be-one Cycling promotion/Dubai, Arbitration Tribunal KNVB, 4 Sep. 2013.
51. HR 12 Aug. 2005, ECLI:NL:HR:2005:AT7337.
52. For example, *see* Art. 53 KNVB, Regulations for professional soccer.
53. Arbitration Tribunal KNVB, 2 Aug. 1977, Mulder S/AZ '67.

some minimum requirements, such as the level of wages, holiday allowances, holidays and the applicable terms of notice. These requirements will be discussed separately.

59. As a result of a European directive, employers are obliged to provide a written statement (except when there is a written employment contract) of the data given below, within one month after the commencement of the employment.[54] This statement has to be signed by the employer. The statement must include, at a minimum:

(a) name and residence of the parties;
(b) place of performance;
(c) description of the position or the nature of labour;
(d) the time of commencement of employment;
(e) in the case of a fixed-term employment contract, the duration of the contract;
(f) the claim to holidays or the means to calculate this claim;
(g) the duration of the terms of notice parties have to comply with or how these terms should be calculated;
(h) the wage and the terms of payment. If the wages depend on the outcome of the labour performed, the amount of labour to be performed each day or week, the price per piece, and the time reasonably involved with the performance;
(i) the usual working hours per day or week;
(j) a statement of whether the employee will participate in a pension scheme;
(k) where an employee works abroad for more than one month, the duration of that labour, the accommodations, the applicability of Dutch social security legislation or the specification of the official bodies concerned with social security legislation, the currency of payment, and the allowances the employee is entitled to and the means of dealing with repatriation;
(l) the applicable CLA or applicable condition based on the Act working through intermediaries (WAADI);
(m) a statement of whether the employment contract is a transfer agreement (*see* paragraph 66 below) or payroll agreement (*see* paragraph 66 below);
(n) if the contract is entered into for an unlimited period of time;
(o) if the contract is an on-call agreement (*see* paragraph 64 below).

60. The employee has to be informed of alterations to the above-mentioned data in writing within one month after the alteration. This does not apply if the alteration results from regulations by law or the applicable CLA. This obligation to write down such a statement does not apply to a person solely performing household or personal labour on behalf of a private person. In that case, the employer has to only comply with this requirement at the employee's request. An employer who refuses to provide this statement or provides an incorrect statement is liable for any damages consequently suffered by the employee. The practical consequences of this are unknown, since there is no known case law on this matter. It could be argued that in that case the burden of proof would also be shifted to the employer.

54. Article 7:655 Civil Code.

61. For the sake of completeness, it should be mentioned that many CLAs already provide a standard written employment contract. Also, regulations of associations often contain a similar stipulation. Next to this, the employer is not allowed to charge the employee for providing this statement or drawing up the employment contract.[55]

C. *Flexible Employment*

62. Dutch labour law is often thought to be rigid. In particular, this is the result of Dutch law on the termination of employment, which will be discussed below. In practice, employers look for ways to be as flexible as possible. Besides a number of statutory possibilities, there are several options which have taken shape in practice. In that connection, it should be pointed out that a flexible construction (whether it is a legal or practical construction) should be chosen only after serious consideration, the more so because misapplication of the regulations concerned can unintentionally entail the formation of an employment contract (for a definite or indefinite period of time) with the employee, which can have grave financial consequences. One can think of legal actions to recover wages (with a possible 50% sanction on top of that amount due to late payment) combined with social security contributions and overdue tax on wages. In other words, this overdue payment can carry a heavy fine.

63. The Dutch legislator has left open the possibility of deviating from particular statutory standard regulations by means of a CLA. However, such deviation is only possible if it is recognized by law. Examples are matters concerning the duration of the probationary period, the applicable term of notice of termination, and the number of fixed-term employment contracts which can be consecutively concluded within a certain period of time. This possibility is often used. The CLA for professional soccer players renders inoperative the statutory restriction to conclude several fixed-term employment contracts within a certain period of time or number of fixed-term employment contracts. This also applies to the (assistant) coach, the technical director, the technical manager, the head coordinator of scouting, the head youth trainer and the specialist trainer (*see* CLA Trainer/Coaches paid football) and the Federal coach or technical director employed by a national sports federation.[56] Notable is the fact that, besides CLAs, there is a possibility to apply for deviation through a request with the Ministry of Social Affairs and Employment. Through this regulation professional football players, coaches, managers, etc. have been excluded from the prohibition to conclude more than three fixed-term contracts.[57]

64. The employment contract itself also leaves open possibility for flexibility as well. Accordingly, the fixed-term employment contract, the employment contract

55. Article 7:654 Civil Code.
56. *See* Art. 7:668a, s. 8 Civil Code; Regeling ketenbepaling bijzondere functie en hogere vergoeding kantonrechter, Stcrt. 2015, 17972.
57. Regeling ketenbepaling voor bijzondere functies en hogere vergoeding kantonrechter.

on-call or an employment contract with a minimum or maximum volume are all possible forms of employment contracts. One should be attentive to the relevant regulations, including the above-mentioned presumptions of law. This issue can be of importance with regard to sponsorship agreements. Under certain circumstances, sponsorship can entail a possible employment relationship between the sporting club and the sportsman. In such a case, the presumptions of law can play a part.[58] After all, it is a matter of payment and performance. To prevent any misunderstanding, the contract should be in writing and the sporting club should arrange it with several sportsmen, resulting in the absence of a relationship of authority. To state explicitly in the sponsorship agreement that an employment contract is not intended is not sufficient. Ultimately, a judge will weigh all relevant facts and circumstances of the relationship.

65. It is possible to conclude an employment contract 'on-call' with the employee. When the volume of labour is less than fifteen hours a week and the working hours are not fixed in advance, the employee is entitled to wages at least equal to three hours of labour, even when the call involves less than three hours of labour.[59] New legislation (Act on Balancing the Labour Market: 'Wab') entered into force on 1 January 2020 regulating, among other subjects, on-call contracts. First of all, a definition of an on-call contract has been included in the law. An on-call contract is a labour contract of which the volume is no fixed number of hours within a month or year. If the contract is an on-call contract the call has to be in writing and at least four days in advance. If the call is four days in advance the employee is obliged to go to work and if the call is cancelled he has no right to any remuneration. In case the call is less than four days in advance the employee can decline and if the call is cancelled the employee retains his right to receive salary for the hours he would have worked if the call had not been cancelled. This term can be deviated from via CLA. Another new obligation since 2020 is to offer an on-call employee a fixed-volume contract after one year, based on the average volume of the past twelve months.

66. There is a possibility of entering into a contract for hiring temporary employees through a temporary employment agency. In the case of such an agreement, the employee enters into employment with an employment agency (the employer) after which the agency assigns the temporary employment agency worker to a principal (the recipient). Usually, the recipient will be able to terminate the employment with the employee without notice. In most cases, the relationship between the employee and the temporary employment agency is provided for by extensive CLA. In most cases, the employment can be terminated without notice for a period of twenty-six weeks which can be extended up to seventy-eight weeks. In practice, the statutory regulations concerned do not provide much protection for the employee.[60]

58. For example, Kantonrechter Heerenveen, 23 Aug. 2000, Sportzaken 2000/3 (No. 15).
59. Article 7:628A Civil Code.
60. Articles 7:690 et seq., Civil Code.

67. It should be pointed out that clubs often assign a sportsman to another club. Usually, the employee has to grant permission for this transfer. The sportsman will be seconded to the recipient club, yet the employee is still employed at his own club. In general, the agreement between both clubs will be labelled a commission contract.[61] The seconding club remains the formal employer. On the other hand, the recipient club is in charge of the employment. This situation is specified in the figure below:

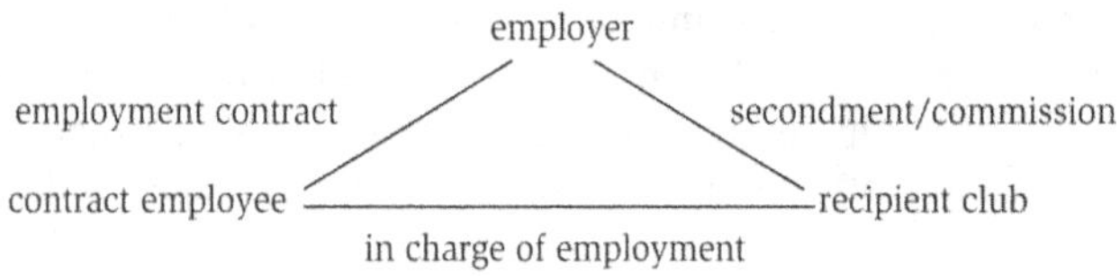

This situation should be based on clear understandings between all of the parties involved. Moreover, the regulations of the associations should be taken into consideration, including regulations concerning transfers. For example, is it possible for a sportsman to play for another club in the course of a competition? And if so, under what conditions?

A special form of the transfer agreement is called a payroll contract. The structure of the collaboration is the same as the above mentioned, with the difference that the formal employer has not actively searched for a suitable employee. In the case of payroll contracts the recipient has searched for an employee and subsequently ordered the payroll company to enter into an employment contract. This is advantageous for the recipient because he does not have the burden of an employment contract but does not have to pay the payroll company for their head-hunting services. In the past this construction has led to situations where payroll employees were paid less than employees who were directly employed by the recipient. This is no longer possible under new legislation. Payroll workers have to receive the same primary, secondary, individual and collective working conditions as workers who are directly employed by the recipient.

D. Medical Examination

68. Dutch law does not allow any general medical examinations. According to the Medical Examinations Act (Wet op de medische keuringen (WMK)) for an employment relationship, disability insurance or pension insurance, questions of a medical nature can only be asked and medical examinations can only be carried out insofar as it is necessary for the intended purpose. In deciding whether the medical examination data is being used for the intended purpose, consideration should be given to the intended work which will be performed. In particular, the medical requirements concerning the position are of importance. Moreover, the obligation to undergo a medical examination has to be mentioned during recruitment. During

61. Article 7:400 Civil Code. For example, *see* Rechtbank Haarlem, 10 Sep. 2002, Sportzaken 2002/4 (No. 24) B1.

such an examination, it is not permitted to ask questions which are disproportionately intrusive and invade the employee's right of privacy. Furthermore, the examination must not involve a disproportionate burden for the employee and it is not permissible to ask questions against the employee's personal interest. Moreover, it is not permissible to ask questions concerning transmissible illness during an insurance examination, unless a certain financial interest is exceeded. The expenses of the examination are to be paid for by the employer.

69. If the above-mentioned statutory conditions are not met, the (prospective) employee is entitled to withhold his participation in the medical examination. In addition, the employee is entitled to a re-examination in the case of an unfavourable medical report. A re-examination should be applied within one week after the employee is notified of the examination results. The above notwithstanding, an employee is obliged to inform his future employer of any medical disabilities which will prevent him from performing his duties.

70. In practice, employment contracts are regularly concluded contingent upon the employee being found medically suitable. Such a condition (if under the legal terms of examination regulations) is allowed. However, since it is a standard customary condition,[62] this contingency must be stipulated explicitly and in writing. In the field of sports, a medical examination is allowed, provided that the medical test requirements are directly related to the physical requirements which have to be fulfilled by the sportsman. Furthermore, internal regulations of the sports association concerned may contain medical test requirements; these requirements are also restricted by the Medical Examinations Act.

71. The called-in medical examiner has to form an opinion on the basis of his own expertise, independently of his client. The medical examiner must conceal the medical data collected and is only allowed to report strictly necessary data to the employer. It is obvious that the examined employee can only apply for a re-examination when the results of the examination become known.

§2. Fundamental Rights and Obligations

I. Right to Work

72. Dutch law does not grant the employee a right to employment. This issue has been discussed several times in NJ and the HR has taken the position that a general right to employment does not exist. Although a general right to employment is not provided for by law, this right has been linked to the concept of 'good employership'[63] and the HR has recognized this right under certain conditions.[64] The lower courts have taken a more extreme position by judging that the employer is under an

62. *See* Arbitration Tribunal KNVB, No. 833, Sportzaken 2001/2 (No. 18) B1A and B1B.
63. Article 7:611 Civil Code.
64. HR 26 Mar. 1965, NJ 1965, 163; HR 27 May 1983, NJ 1983/758; HR 12 May 1989, NJ 1989/801.

obligation to provide the employee with employment. In that case, too, the legal foundation is the concept of 'good employership'. This is different only in case the employer can prove the employee's misconduct or lack of diligence.

73. The right to employment is essentially connected with cooperation with the sporting association and the team. The right and obligation to participate in games, competitions and tournaments is conditional upon the employer's and employee's requirements and mutual agreement. In membership relations or comparable legal relations, the right to participate is generally viewed to be voluntary, which is the foundation of these relations.[65] It is inherent in the practice of sports to restrict, both in membership relations and in contractual relations, participation in sporting competitions by the same requirements, which are inextricably bound up with the practice of sports.

74. These restrictions on the right to employment can be divided into three categories:

- The first category of restrictions results from the requirements of the game itself, included in the rules of play and the regulations regarding competitions and the equal and fair circumstances under which this game will take place.
- The second category of restrictions results from the requirements in sports for the rivalry underlying the game and the (monopolistic) structure of sports built on that basis.
- The third category of restrictions results from the requirements in sports for their social status.[66]

75. The Arbitral Tribunal KNVB has taken the position that the employer must provide employment to the employee (sportsman and trainer).[67] Therefore, the right to work is, in principle, acknowledged in sports. Taking specific circumstances into consideration, one should decide whether or not continuing the performed activities (whether or not in the same function) is advisable and in the parties' best interest. Only when urgent reasons militate against the employment, can an exception to the right to work be made. In this respect, one can also argue whether or not there is a right to play.[68] Such a right could originate from membership in the sports club. In this regard, it should be taken into account that a team usually consists of more players than can actually be played on the field. This would mean that the club has the right to reduce the number of sportsmen selected to play, as long as this reduction is based on objective justifiable grounds and the players are all treated equally. According to case law, a distinction should be made between the right to participate in training on the one hand, and the right to play in matches, on the other.

---

65. F.C. Kollen & H.T. van Staveren, *Sport en recht*, deel 8, 2000, 34.
66. *Ibid.*, 35.
67. Arbitration Tribunal KNVB, 29 Jan. 1975 Wullems/NAC, President of the Court Amsterdam, 3 Apr. 1975, NJ 1975, 285.
68. Arbitration Tribunal KNVB, No. 136.

76. Dutch law is highly influenced by European law, in particular with regard to the freedom of employees. All residents of any Member State of the EU have the right to travel freely between all states of the Union and to be employed there. A host state may not in any way treat foreign employees differently from its national employees. On the other hand, an employee with a nationality from a state which is not a member of the EU cannot base any claim on EU law.

77. Not using a player can lead to termination of the employee's labour contract. Furthermore, not allowing a player to work could be considered a wrongful act committed against this player. In such a case, the employee can claim damages from the employer. Subsequently substantiating the extent of the damages appears to be up to the employee. Based on case law, not only lost income is taken into account, but indirect damages that result from negative publicity and the closely connected defamation of character of the employee/player as well.[69]

78. It should be mentioned that not allowing an employee to work, or not letting him play in a match, does not mean the employer is not obligated to pay him wages. After all, the employee/player is available to perform labour. Therefore, the obligation to continue payment of wages remains in full force. The same reasoning applies, to some extent, when a player is suspended.[70] According to case law, the only exception arises if the employment contract explicitly states that in such a situation payment of wages may be discontinued.

II. Freedom of Association

79. In the Netherlands, the right of freedom of association is recognized. This right has been laid down in Article 8 of the Constitution and can be restricted only in the interests of public order. This right must be viewed in conjunction with the right of freedom of speech and freedom of assembly. Trade union members are protected under these rights as well. The association is a legal entity consisting of members with a common goal. It is provided for in the second chapter of the second book of the Dutch BW. The common goal may not be a stipulation of profit. To avoid liability for individual members, associations are founded by notarial deed. Restrictions of freedoms in the interest of the public order must be interpreted conservatively – for example, engaging in criminal activities would meet this restrictive interpretation. Freedom of Association gives people not only the right to joins clubs, but also constitutes the right for these clubs to exclude certain people from membership. Membership of a club arises from mutual consent, so in principle the sports club decides whether or not to allow someone to become a member and cannot be forced to admit someone. Under special circumstances a denial of membership can be a breach of unwritten law. Primarily when there is no good reason for the denial

69. Arbitration Tribunal KNVB, No. 373.
70. D. Schwartz, 'Loondoorbetalingsplicht bij geschorste sporters. Tuchtrechtelijke schorsingen *all in the game?*', *TvS&R* 2020, 3/4.

and obtaining the membership, the membership is of great importance for the specific person. This was made clear in respect to sports clubs by the Court of Appeal in a case concerning a sports shooter who wished to become a member of a shooting association but was denied membership because of his criminal behaviour in the past. The Court of Appeals judged the shooting association was not obliged to grant him membership.[71]

III. Freedom of Speech

80. The Netherlands respects freedom of speech. This right is anchored in international treaties as well as in Article 7 of the Constitution. This right is not limited to any particular medium, such as radio, newspapers, television and the internet. There is no preliminary inquiry that must be made with regard to the content to be disseminated by the media. Freedom of speech is restricted only by individual responsibility; consequently, an utterance will not be protected if it may be harmful to another person. Criminal law restricts freedom of speech in a number of cases.

IV. Right to Privacy and Image Rights

81. The legislation on privacy in the Netherlands is a direct effect of European legislation. The legislation in question can be found in the European GDPR. The core objective of this act is that personal data can only be registered and used for the essential purposes of its collection. Furthermore, it is not permissible to store such data any longer than strictly necessary. Additionally, it is prohibited to store especially sensitive personal data. Such data concerns religion, race, political disposition, health, sexual life, membership of a trade union or information on criminal history. The keeper of the data is obliged to store the acquired data in a secure place and inform the person whose privacy has been invaded, unless it is a matter of statutory obligation. Subsequently the person concerned also has the right to look at the data and to make changes, if necessary. Moreover, it has been pointed out that a works council may have a right of consent if the registered person does not agree with the means of registration. The works council can then bring the case to court or before the Data Protection Board.

V. Equal Opportunities[72]

82. According to Article 1 of the Constitution, everyone must be treated equally in the Netherlands. This fundamental right is also acknowledged in many treaties. Moreover, the EU has also been active in the field of equal treatment. This has resulted in a number of EU directives being introduced into national legislation by

71. Hof Arnhem-Leeuwarden, 14 May 2019, ECLI:NL:GHARL:2019:4168.
72. P.C. Vas Nunes, *Gelijke behandeling in Arbeid*, Den Haag 2018.

the Member States, among them the Netherlands. The foundation for this legislation is the Equal Treatment Act. This act prohibits the employer from discriminating on the basis of religion, belief, political disposition, race, sex, nationality, hetero- or homosexual orientation or marital status. This norm applies to everybody. However, discrimination is allowed in two cases. In case of positive discrimination, people may be discriminated against in order to create a balance between different groups of people, for instance, women or people with a different ethnic or cultural background. The second occasion where a discrimination is allowed is when a particular gender is decisive for performing a duty, for example, in the case of a priest or an actor. An example of possible discrimination arose in a case about a dancing couple. The couple consisted of two men. The couple wanted to participate in national amateur dancing competitions. The Dutch Amateur Dance Federation (NADB) stated that the couple could not participate because a couple should consist of a man and a woman. The couple argued that they were being discriminated against on the basis of gender. The judge agreed with the NADB, stating that the male couple may be excluded from the national games insofar as there is a difference between the average performance of men and women. This is the case in the area of sports.[73]

83. In the Netherlands, equal treatment legislation is also reflected in the labour law. It is prohibited to make a distinction between men and women when entering into an employment contract, as well as during the duration of the contract and when the contract is terminated.[74] Equal treatment can only be ignored when there is an objective justification. Making a distinction between employees in connection with their working hours, or because they have a fixed-term employment contract as opposed to a contract for an indefinite period of time, is also prohibited.[75] In determining whether there is discrimination, a distinction is made between direct and indirect discrimination. Direct discrimination means that the discrimination is directly related to the status of the person, for example, a pregnant woman. This form of discrimination is strictly prohibited. In the case of indirect discrimination, the discriminatory action, to a lesser degree, results in discrimination against a certain group of people. The last-mentioned form of discrimination is only permissible when the employer can prove that there is an objective ground of justification which is not connected with the discrimination itself.

84. Furthermore, Dutch legislation prohibits discrimination against potential employees based on a disability caused by age (*Wet gelijke behandeling op grond van leeftijd bij arbeid* (WGBL)) unless the discrimination can be justified on objective grounds. Especially in sports, distinctions based on age have serious consequences. This problem arose in a case involving Dutch soccer referees whose employment contract contained a provision stating that their contract would terminate when they reached the age of 47 years. The KNVB stated that there was an

---

73. A.E.L. Rehbock & A.J. van Dijk, '*Overzicht gelijkebehandelingswetgeving*', Arbeidsrecht 2005 – 5 nr. 29. *And* Rechtbank Den Haag 26 Jul. 2006, JIN 2007/35.
74. Article 7:646 Civil Code.
75. Articles 7:648 and 7:649 Civil Code.

objective justification, because older referees were not able to meet the required high physical and mental standards. The court ruled that this was a matter of forbidden distinction since there was no objective justification. The KNVB had other options available to objectively test the physical and mental condition of the referees. It can only be on the basis of these test results that the referees' physical and mental condition may be judged.[76]

Another law legislating equal treatment is the Equal Treatment for Men and Women Act (*Wet gelijke behandeling mannen en vrouwen* (WGB)). This act was created to implement Article 141 EC – treaty and the directives concerning equal treatment. The basic rule states that direct and indirect discrimination based on gender is forbidden. The exception to the rule is for indirect discrimination, if there is an objective justification.[77]

The burden of proof is treated differently in case of discrimination. The person who claims to have been discriminated against must show facts which make this statement likely to be true. The opposing party must prove that there was no sign of discrimination and that he did not act against the equal treatment legislation.[78]

In conclusion, it must be mentioned that the Supreme Court has stated that good employership generally includes equal pay for equal work.[79] Salary should be taken into account as well as the above-mentioned regulations on discrimination. Experience teaches us that judges are slow to implement this universal right. Moreover, the obligation to prove that there is a factual matter of unequal pay for equal work rests with the employee.[80]

VI. Civil and Criminal Liability

85. In the course of working, accidents may occur, even if all the legal provisions concerned, like good employership and the Working Conditions Act, have been complied with. Furthermore, Article 7:658 BW explicitly states that the employer is obliged to organize work as far as reasonably possible in such a way as to prevent harm to the employee. The law states that the employer is liable to the employee for any damage the latter may suffer during the performance of labour, unless the employer can prove that he has done everything reasonably possible to fulfil his obligations or in case the damage has been caused intentionally or by the deliberate recklessness of the employee. To avoid liability, the employer must prove that he has done everything necessary to provide proper working conditions. In doing so, he should take into account the fact that an employee may occasionally

76. A.E.L. Rehbock & A.J. van Dijk, '*Overzicht gelijkebehandelingswetgeving*', Arbeidsrecht 2005 – 5 nr. 29. *And* Hof Amsterdam 13 Jan. 2000, NJ 2000/466.
77. A.E.L. Rehbock & A.J. van Dijk, '*Overzicht gelijkebehandelingswetgeving*', Arbeidsrecht 2005 – 5 nr. 29.
78. *Ibid.*
79. HR 8 Apr. 1994, NJ 1994, 704, AGFA and HR 30 Jan. 2004, RvdW 2004, 26.
80. On this subject: D.J.B. de Wolff, *Gelijk loon voor gelijke arbeid: de toepassing van een beginsel in de rechtspraktijk*, SR 2003, 105 et seq., *see also*: A.G. Veldman, '*Goed werkgeverschap en gelijk loon voor gelijke arbeid*', Arbeid Integraal 2008, 37 et seq.

neglect his duties. This obligation is imposed partly by the Working Conditions Act. The employer will generally not be liable if neglect by the worker can be proved.

86. Moreover, in case law, the employer's liability is regularly extended on the basis of good employership. This concerns accidents which are related to labour, but do not actually occur during the performance of that labour. An example of this is accidents occurring in commuter traffic or accidents after-hours. In that case all circumstances must be taken into consideration to determine whether the employer is liable, based on, for instance, good employership. If the employer is viewed to be responsible, he will have to pay damages.

87. Next to damage to the employee, there is the possibility of an employee causing damage to his employer or to property belonging to a third party during the performance of labour. In this case, the employee is generally not liable; it is the employer who is considered to bear the risk of such damage. This is different only when the damage is caused intentionally or through the deliberate recklessness of the employee. Circumstances may also result in a different apportionment of damage. Considering the fact that it is the employer who must prove the intention or deliberate recklessness of the employee, the liability of the employee is not easily established. In any case, a single moment of inattention by the employee is insufficient to prove recklessness. To provide the full picture, it should be pointed out that in most cases the employer will carry liability insurance.

§3. Employment Regulation

I. Contractual Rights and Obligations

A. Wages

88. The employer is obliged to pay the employee wages.[81] Alternative ways of payment include:

- the provision of products for personal use provided that this is common or desirable for the enterprise concerned, with the exception of alcohol or drugs;
- the free use of a house (including electricity and water);
- the performance of services by or on account of the employer, the making of arrangements or the performance of work;
- securities and claims.

In case of payment in kind, the law prescribes that the payment is to be valued at the actual cost.

81. Article 7:617 Civil Code.

89. As a starting point, the extent of the wages is agreed upon by the parties themselves. When this does not happen, wages customary for the performed activities are due and if no customary wages for comparable activities exist, the wages must be fair.[82] In such a case, the applicable CLA or a comparable CLA is taken into consideration; research is often conducted for this purpose.[83] The extent of wages is subject to a statutory minimum under the Minimum Wage and Minimum Holiday Allowance Act. According to the situation, from 1 January 2021, the statutory minimum wages are as set forth immediately below in Table 2.

Table 2 Legal Gross Youth Minimum Wages as from 1 July 2021 (EUR)

Age	*Standard Minimum Wage*	*Monthly*	*Weekly*	*Daily*
From 21 years	100	1,701.00	392.55	78.51
20 years	61.5	1,360.80	314.05	62.81
19 years	52.5	1,020.60	235.55	47.11
18 years	45.5	850.50	196.30	39.26
17 years	39.5	671.90	155.05	31.01
16 years	34.5	586.85	135.45	27.09
15 years	30	510.30	117.75	23.55

These amounts are revised twice a year.[84] The minimum youth wage starts at the age of 15 years. The Supreme Court has decided in 2006 that there should not be a minimum wage for 13- and 14-year-olds. The court stated that it is more important for those children to go to school than to start working.[85] Recently the age on which an employee receives the highest minimum wage has been lowered from 23 to 21 years.

90. As a result of the contractual obligations the employer only owes wages when the employee is available to carry out work. If the employee refuses to carry out the work assigned, the employer has no obligation to pay wages. Furthermore, the employer will have to continue paying wages when the work is not carried out in a situation for which the employer bears the risk. An example of this is weather conditions. Illness and care leave are also examples of this exception, but these will be discussed below, since specific provisions apply to these situations. Generally, payments have to be made within one week after the period in which the payment was earned.[86] The employer is obliged to provide a pay slip containing, among other things, a gross/net calculation.[87] When payment of the wages is (partly) dependent

82. Article 7:618 Civil Code.
83. *See*, for example, 'BDO, Nationale beloningsonderzoek voor hockeytrainers 2001'.
84. For the most recent amounts *see* www.rijksoverheid.nl.
85. HR 10 Nov. 2006, C05/133HR; ECLI:NL:HR:2006:AY9216.
86. Article 7:623 Civil Code.
87. Article 7:626 Civil Code and the Minimum Wage and Minimum Holiday Allowance Act.

upon certain data, for instance, the turnover that was made, the employee has the right to examine these data.[88] The law imposes a sanction if the employer is late in making payments, in which case the employee is entitled to extra pay due to the delay. Per day, this amounts to:

- four to eight days: 5%;
- every day thereafter: 1%;
- the fine can mount up to a maximum of 50%.

91. Moreover, the employee is entitled to statutory interest as per the date that the right to wages became due. Prior notice of default is not required for the indebtedness of the employer. The claim to statutory interest arises by law and it currently amounts to 2%. For the sake of completeness it is pointed out that the court is free to moderate the fine in an equitable fashion in the light of circumstances. Experience shows that this happens frequently (usually limiting the fine to 10%).[89]

B. Good Employeeship and Good Employership

92. In accordance with Article 7:611 BW, the employer is obliged to behave towards the employee in the way that a good employer should behave. Likewise, the employee is obliged to behave as a good employee. As appears from case law, these obligations are far-reaching, but above all of a factual nature. Related to the specific situation it must be judged what a 'good employee' or a 'good employer' should reasonably have done under the given circumstances. This obligation should be taken into consideration constantly. Examples from case law of good employership include:

- the employer must provide a safe workplace;
- an employee unfit for work must be enabled (as far as possible) to perform his work (or adjusted work), and the employer can be expected to adjust the employee's duties and/or workplace, within reasonable limits.

Examples of good employeeship include the below:

- the employee is obliged to handle the property of the employer with care;
- in case of incidental pressure of business, the employee should work overtime;
- the employee should react with a positive attitude to a proposal from the employer to adjust his employment contract and he may not turn down the proposal on unfounded grounds.

88. Article 7:619 Civil Code.
89. M.W.A.M. van Kempen, '*De wettelijke verhoging ex art. 7:625 BW en de black box van de matiging*', TAP 2019/5.

In practice, the effect of these concepts should not be underestimated. Again and again, this concept must be given content according to all relevant facts and circumstances. Although case law on this subject is of a casuistic nature, the courts are usually willing to extend the scope of employership, especially insofar as it determines what may be expected from a good employer.

The training requirement [scholingsplicht] is a statutory elaboration of good employership of the employer. On this basis, the employer must allow the employee to follow training which is necessary for the performance of his duties as far as it may be required by the employer for the continuation of the labour agreement. This training requirement is linked to the expiry of the function of the employee or the inability of the employee to fulfil it.[90]

II. (Non-) Competition/Exclusivity

93. Under Dutch law, it is possible to include non-competition clauses in an employment contract for fixed-term employment contracts, and such a clause is only possible if it is in writing. The employer has to demonstrate the necessity of the clause.[91] The law states that, in principle, it is prohibited to include a non-competition clause in a fixed-term contract, unless there is a specific reason for it and this reason is explicitly explained in the contract. A stipulation which affects the right of the employee to be in any way employed elsewhere after the employment contract has come to an end is only valid when there is a written stipulation, concluded with an employee of age 18 years or more.[92] In that case, the employee will, in general, be bound to the non-competition clause. There is a possibility though that the court will nullify the clause partially or completely. As a criterion, a weighing up of interests is used as well as the question of whether or not the employee is restricted in an unreasonable way. Moreover, the court may decide that although the clause may remain in effect, the employer is obliged to pay reasonable compensation.

As appears from case law, the courts assess these restrictions critically. In addition, it is the employer who must prove the existence of a legitimate interest. A legitimate interest is often assumed to exist when the employee has been trained (beyond the norm) by the employer and/or when the employee possesses specific information concerning his employer's enterprise, among which may be information concerning clients. The judge will then still attempt to limit the scope of the non-competition clause, either in territory and/or in time. A non-competition clause may be limited to a stipulation concerning clients, in connection with an obligation of confidentiality.

An agreed-on competition clause can lose its validity in the course of the work relationship. Employees frequently undergo a serious function modification, with

90. Article 7:611A Civil Code.
91. Article 7:653, s. 2 Civil Code.
92. Article 7:653 Civil Code.

preservation of the current employment contract. The consequence of such a function modification can be that the existing non-competition clause has an increased negative impact on the employee: it will be more difficult to find a new comparable job.

The judge grants weight to the degree in which the function modification was reasonably foreseeable for the employee at the time the non-competition clause was agreed upon. The judge must not only assess whether or not there is a serious function modification; he must also judge if the non-competition clause forms a larger obstacle to the employee to find a new comparable job, due to the function modification.

In short, the non-competition clause is included in Article 7:653 BW and the following elements are of importance:

- in principle non-competition clauses in fixed-term contracts are not allowed;
- to be valid the non-competition clause has to be in writing, agreed between an employer and an employee;
- a judge can terminate the clause partly or fully void if the employee is unfairly disadvantaged compared to the protected interests of the employee;
- the employer cannot deriver any rights to the clause if he has caused any damage. This is the case when the employee has been dismissed instantaneously without urgent reason or when the employee has not observed his term of notice;
- if a clause restricts an employee, a judge can decide that the employer has to pay a compensation for the time the deterrent lasts. The employer is not bound to pay this compensation when the employee seems to be liable for compensation.

The law does not provide a maximum period for a non-competition clause. However, in general, the periods used in practice lie between one and two years maximum. If this period is longer, it will most often be modified by the judge. In addition, it is of importance to make this period as concrete as possible and to resemble this period to the time it takes in which the knowledge of the employee will lose its value.

The non-competition clause can, next to the above-mentioned, be applicable for a specific region or for the whole country. Parties have no limitation when making such arrangements. When deciding on the distance of the region the function and activities of the employee are primarily of importance. Here too the advice pertains to specify the region as clearly as possible and to make the region not too large. It is of importance by specifying the region to try to limit it to the region where the major clients are located.

Furthermore, the functional or business range is important. This contains a definition of the activities an employee is not allowed to execute after termination of the employment. According to literature and according to the advice of the chamber of commerce it is advised to limit this to specific situations. If the definition is too broad, the judge has the competency to modify or even terminate the non-competition clause.

The non-competition clause ought to be as clear and specific as possible in its wording and limitations, but must not be unreasonably unfair towards the employee. The unfairness of the non-competition clause can be reviewed afterwards by a judge. A non-competition clause is unfair when the admission to the free labour market would be denied.[93] In addition, the circumstances of the case will be weighed.[94] Also when the non-competition clause is not directly harming the employee, but when the employer has no interest in preserving the clause, the clause can be modified by the judge.[95]

Because of the strict limitations for competition-clauses in fixed-term contracts, they are rarely seen in contracts with athletes. After all they are usually employed on the basis of fixed-term contracts.

A. *Education-Cost Clause*

94. An employee is free to work for a new employer; however, under Dutch case law this right can be restricted by an existing education-cost clause. It is possible to include an education-cost clause in an employment contract concerning liability for the educational costs in case of termination of the employment contract. It defines the period of time wherein the former employee is obliged to refund (part of) the employer's investment in the employee's educational costs. The education-cost clause enables the employer to hold on to employees in whom he invested experience, skills and knowledge. The range of refunding may vary from solely the costs of study to the wages paid during the period of education. The scope of the refund is unrelated to the actual costs of the education.

The Supreme Court has set three main requirements for a valid education-cost clause. The first requirement is the limitation of the period of time at which the employer is anticipated to benefit from the knowledge and skills gained as a result of the employee's education. The second condition is the determination of the employee's obligation to refund wages to the employer in case the employment contract comes to an end during or immediately after the educational period. The third condition is the proportional decrease of the refund obligation during a fixed period of time.[96]

The education-cost clause also involves other limitations. Particular sections of Dutch law (for instance, the *Wet Minimumloon en Minimumvakantiebijslag*) can place boundaries on what parties can agree to. The phrasing and explanation of the education-cost clause must be very clear, because of the drastic consequences it can have for the employee. Keeping an employee to the education-cost clause can be unreasonable, under certain circumstances, if the employer initiated the termination of the employment contract.[97] The unreasonableness of the obligation depends on the particular circumstances.[98]

---

93. Sector kanton rechtbank Arnhem 7 Aug. 2008, ECLI:NL:RBARN:2007:BB2022.
94. Gerechtshof Leeuwarden 11 Jun. 2003, ECLI:NL:GHLEE:2003:AG0200.
95. Rechtbank Breda, 18 Aug. 2010, ECLI:NL:RBBRE:2010:BN4208.
96. HR 10 Jun. 1983, NJ 1983, 796 (Muller/Van Opzeeland).
97. HR 10 Jun 1983, NJ 1983, 796 (Muller/ Van Opzeeland); Loonstra & Zondag 2005, 477–481.
98. W.H. van Aalst, '*Het studiekostenbeding nogmaals bestudeerd*', Arbeidsrecht 2004/1, 22, *see also* O.J. Rote, '*Het studiekostenbeding*', Arbeidsrecht 2011/58.

The obligation to repay must be explicitly described in the education-cost clause.[99] A reference in the employment contract to an education-cost clause that is incorporated in a general education-cost regulation is valid.[100] In that case the employer must notify the employee explicitly about any costs that arise from any specific education. Any possible obscurities concerning the education-cost clause are interpreted to the detriment of the employer. The education-cost clause is interpreted as limitedly as possible.[101]

In sports, education-cost clauses can be desirable when high costs and time investment has been put into the training of an athlete. In football these costs are integrated within the transfer sum so education-cost clauses are rarely seen in this sector of sports.

III. Disciplinary Actions

95. This discussion deals with the question as to what extent an employee may be denied admission to his workplace and other disciplinary actions. In fact, there are two options for punishing an employee: suspension and forced garden leave. Suspension is often regarded as a disciplinary action and may be accompanied by suspension of pay. In that case, the suspension may have been imposed awaiting the outcome of, for example, an investigation that may lead to definitive punitive measures, among which may be dismissal. Giving 'leave' relates to the discharge of the employee from his duty to work, for example, if a certain position is terminated as a result of reorganization, the employee is relieved of his duty to work while awaiting the dismissal procedure.

96. In determining the legitimacy of these possibilities, all the relevant circumstances must be taken into consideration. Relevant data, for instance, as incorporated in the collective bargaining agreement, staff manual, employment contract or the disciplinary provisions laid down in the law of associations, can play a role in this determination. Furthermore, the employer will have to act as a good employer and is not allowed to unilaterally cease/defer payment of wages as a punitive action. To take this action legally, it is necessary that the right to cease/defer payment is

99. Ktr. Eindhoven 11 Oct. 2001, Prg. 2001, nr. 5771.

100. Ktr. Eindhoven 11 Oct. 2001, Prg. 2001, nr. 5771; Ktg. Zaandam 1 Nov. 2001, JAR 2001, 249; Ktr. Eindhoven 13 Dec. 2007, Prg. 2002, 5854; Ktr. Rotterdam 7 May 2002, JAR 2002, 182; Ktr. Amsterdam 22 Nov. 2002, JAR 2002, 22; Ktr. Amsterdam 7 Jan. 2003, JAR 2003, 45; Hof Amsterdam 26 Feb. 2004, JAR 2004, 202; Ktr. Rotterdam 1 Oct. 2004, JAR 2004, 69; Ktr. Dordrecht 24 Aug. 2006, ECLI:NL:RBDOR:2006: AY6951; Hof 's-Gravenhage 29 Sep. 2006, JAR 2006, 282; Ktr. Rotterdam 28 Feb. 2007, *Prg.* 2007, 64; Ktr. Leeuwarden 4 Oct. 2007, ECLI:NL:RBLEE:2007:BB6025; Hof Amsterdam 29 May 2008, RAR 2008, 147; Ktr. Haarlem 9 Jul. 2008, JAR 2008, 303; Ktr. Utrecht 18 Mar. 2009, JAR 2009, 137; Ktr. Rotterdam 26 Aug. 2009, JAR 2009, 241; Ktr. Utrecht 23 Jun. 2010, Prg. 2010, 165; Vzr. Rb. Heerenveen 10 Oct. 2010, JAR 2011, 28; Hof Arnhem 8 Mar. 2011, ECLI:NL:GHARN:2011:BQ1355; Hof 's-Gravenhage 22 Mar. 2011, ECLI:NL:GHSGR:2011:BQ3253; Vzr. Rb. Dordrecht 5 Apr. 2011, *JAR* 2011, 118; Ktr. Harderwijk 29 Feb. 2012, JAR 2012, 98; Ktr. Amersfoort 29 Jul. 2015, ECLI:NL:RBMNE:2015:5474; Hof Leeuwarden 8 Sep. 2015, ECLI:NL:GHARL:2015:6643.

101. O.J. Rote, '*Het studiekostenbeding*', Arbeidsrecht 2011/58.

agreed to in writing by both parties, for instance, in the employment contract or collective bargaining agreement.[102] When there is no written agreement, withholding of pay during suspension is not allowed. This does not, however, affect the right to suspend an employee, provided that this is exercised proportionally. In all these situations, the principle of proportionality plays a major role. The suspension/placing on leave must be in proportion to the event and the interests of the employee.[103] Ultimately, the permissibility of the suspension must be examined considering all relevant facts and circumstances.

In sport an extraordinary situation can arise when an athlete is suspended for violating the rules of the sport. Disciplinary action is then usually taken by the sports association and the situation can occur that an athlete is no longer allowed to play matches for a certain period of time. Does the employer have to keep paying the employee during the time he is not allowed to play due to disciplinary actions taken by the sports association? In the view of the authors this is generally the case. In general, foul play or violations of the rules can be considered as part of the (risk of) game, and therefore within the sphere of risk of the employer. Only in certain cases, i.e., a severe and deliberate violation of the rules, this can be viewed differently. In these cases one could argue that the employee is not entitled to remuneration for the time he is being suspended.[104]

97. Under certain circumstances, the employer is given the possibility by Dutch law to impose a fine on the employee as a punitive action. This is, however, only allowed when both parties have agreed to it in writing.[105] It must also be previously defined which offence is punishable by which fine. When the employee is entitled to only minimum wages, the indebtedness of a fine must be mentioned in the employment contract. In that case, the fine must be to the benefit of a goal other than the employer, such as a charitable institution, like Amnesty International or the staff association. Moreover, the fine cannot amount to more than half the employee's daily pay. The court has the option at its disposal to mitigate the fine if it appears excessive. Generally, the court has the possibility to mitigate the fine in any case.[106]

98. Collecting a fine replaces the employer's right to claim damages for the same fact. It is only possible to claim damages when no fine has been claimed and vice versa.[107] Again and again, an employer will have to make a well-considered choice. Moreover, an employer may consider other sanctions, such as a verbal or written warning or (ultimately) instant dismissal. An employer may also sanction his employee when he misbehaves; imposing the sanction must be necessary in order

102. HR 21 Mar. 2003, JAR 2003/91.
103. *See*, for example, President of the Court Haarlem, 27 Apr. 1979, NJ 1980, 52 and President of the Court Utrecht, 18 Sep. 2001, Sportzaken 2001/2 (No. 18) B3; Rechtbank Utrecht 28 Nov. 2011, ECLI:NL:RBUTR:2012:BY4350.
104. D. Schwartz, '*Loondoorbetalingsverplichting bij geschorste sporters. Tuchtrechtelijke schorsingen* all in the game*?*', TvS&R 2020, 1/2.
105. Article 7:650 Civil Code.
106. Articles 6:91–6:94 Civil Code.
107. Article 7:651 Civil Code.

to end the unwanted behaviour. When the employer decides to sanction his employee, he should consider the criminal concepts of '*ne bis in idem*' (double jeopardy) and 'no punishment without guilt'. In sports, most employees are members of a sporting association (and perhaps a sports club). The disciplinary rules of these associations may also impose a fine on the sportsman. The literature on labour law does not provide clarity whether the professional sportsman is, in such a case, protected under the above-mentioned labour law regulations.

IV. Termination of Contract

A. *In General*

99. An employment contract can end in several ways. For example, this can occur by:

- expiration;
- notice of termination;
- mutual agreement;
- dissolution by the court.

B. *Expiration*

100. An employment contract may be concluded for a definite period of time. In that situation, the employment contract ends by operation of law as soon as the agreed period expires.[108] This could involve a specific period of time, for instance, a year, but also a clearly defined event, such as the duration of the illness of an employee who is replaced by the new employee, the time needed for the construction of a building, etc. Usually, an agreement contains a specific period of time. It is not possible under Dutch law to conclude an unlimited number of employment contracts for a fixed period of time. This restriction may be overcome by CLA for specified functions.[109]

This, for example, involves:

- a football player who is registered as a contract player at the professional football section of the KNVB for participation in the men's league of the professional football section;
- a trainer-coach, assistant trainer-coach, technical director, technical manager, scouting chief, scouting coordinator, youth programme chief and trainer specialists, working in professional football;
- the ice hockey player employed by the club Tilburg Trappers.

108. Article 7:667 Civil Code.
109. Article 7:668a, s. 8 Civil Code. Consult Regeling ketenbepaling bijzondere functies en hogere vergoeding kantonrechter, *Stcrt.* 2015, 17972.

101. As a starting principle, the employer is free to conclude a maximum of three employment contracts for a fixed period of time, such as three employment contracts for the length of one year, but also three contracts for the length of one month. The fourth employment contract is deemed to be concluded for an indefinite period of time. It is not possible to circumvent this regulation by repeatedly having the employee enter into the service of a purportedly different employer. Employers who – in all reasonableness – should be regarded as each other's successors are included in the calculation.[110] Temporary employment agencies are also taken into consideration.

102. The employer must inform the employee, who is working on the basis of a temporary employment contract, a month before the agreed period ends about whether and under what conditions the employment relation continues. That obligation does not apply to contracts which last for less than six months or in which it has been agreed that it ends at a time, not being a calendar date. When the employer does not conform to the obligation, he is obliged to compensate the damage by paying a one months' salary. When the employer does conform to the obligation, but not at the right time, he owes a pro rata compensation.[111]

When the employee continues his work after expiration of the agreed period, the employment contract is deemed to have continued under the same conditions and for the same period of time up to a maximum of one year.[112] This means that the employment contract will terminate automatically when this period comes to an end. The foregoing does, however, mean that there is also a possibility to conclude an employment contract for more than three years. Such a contract comes to an end by operation of law, and, in principle, cannot be renewed. In that situation, ordinarily, an employment contract for an indefinite period of time comes into being. Under Dutch law there is, however, one small escape hatch. This involves the possibility to extend the employment contract for one last time for a maximum period of three months.[113] As mentioned above, these regulations may be varied in a CLA; one should always check closely whether or not this is the case. Especially in CLA in sports, the possibility to deviate is often utilized.

C. Notice of Termination

103. According to the legislator, the notice of termination is the main method of termination of the employment contract. The notice of termination requires a legal act of the employer or the employee. The notice of termination may relate to a direct termination of the employment contract or to a long-term termination. For the notice of termination, the law gives prescriptions and other deviating regulations in CLAs.

104. The employer must have a *reasonable ground* for the notice of termination.

110. Article 7:668a Civil Code.
111. Article 7:668, ss 1–2 Civil Code.
112. Article 7:668, ss 3–4. Civil Code.
113. Article 7:668a, s. 3 Civil Code.

Reasonable grounds are:

- business economic circumstances;
- long-term inability to work due to illness (two years illness without any chance of recovery within six months);
- frequent absence due to illness;
- a culpable act or neglect of duty of the employee;
- dysfunction;
- a refusal to work on the basis of conscientious objections;
- a disturbed employment relationship;
- circumstances whereby it is not reasonable to continue the labour agreement;
- a sum of the circumstances mentioned in two or more of the above-mentioned grounds, which lead to a situation where it is no longer reasonable for the employer to continue the contract; and
- reaching the pensionable age.

In addition, reinstatement of the employee, whether using other appropriate training for another function, is not possible or cannot reasonably be required by the employer.

Also, the employer must have a written permission for the notice of termination. When the written permission of the employee is missing, the notice of termination can be given with the permission of the *Uitvoeringsinstituut Werknemersverzekeringen* (UWV) by business economic grounds and long-term disability or abolishment by the kantonrechter in case of other personal reasons. The employee can request the kantonrechter to annihilate the notice of termination or provide him a reasonable indemnity in case the employer does not comply with the conditions.

Finally, the employer must give the notice of termination in writing. The employee can request the kantonrechter to annihilate the notice of termination or provide him a reasonable indemnity in case the employer ends the labour agreement without a notice of termination.[114]

105. When none of the above-mentioned circumstances applies, or in case parties do not wish to go to court or follow a UWV-procedure, termination can be agreed upon by both parties. The employee can withdraw the approval within fourteen days without justification needed. The employer must indicate him on the right, and if not, the revocation period will be extended to three weeks. The employee may use this right only once every six months.

106. The employee who has been given notice during the probation period can, however, claim insight into the reason for the termination.[115]

107. In principle, the termination takes place at the end of the month; one can differ from this rule in writing or by custom.[116] Moreover, in case of termination by

114. Article 7:681 Civil Code.
115. Article 7:676, s. 2 Civil Code.
116. Article 7:672, s. 1 Civil Code.

the employer as well as the employee, one should consider the applicable period of notice of one month. For the employer the period of notice depends on the duration of the employment contract (Table 3).[117] The elapsed period by getting the permission for the termination can be deducted from the applicable period of notice.[118]

Table 3 Applicable Period of Notice for the Employer Depending on the Duration of the Contracts

Duration of the Contract and Period of Notice	*Duration of Contract Period of Notice*
5 years or less	1 month
Between 5 and 10 years	2 months
Between 10 and 15 years	3 months
More than 15 years	4 months

The notice period for an employee is – in principle – one month.[119]

In a CLA, these periods of notice can be varied. It is possible, as well, for parties to vary these notices in writing. This, however, is only possible if the period of notice for the employee does not exceed six months and if the period of notice for the employer doubles the period of notice for the employee. Furthermore, it should be pointed out that an employment contract for a fixed period of time can only be terminated prematurely if both parties have previously agreed to this in writing.[120]If the employer does not comply with the applicable notice period, the employee can request the *kantonrechter* to grant a compensation which is equal to the salary that should have been paid if the employer had complied with the applicable notice period.[121] In conclusion, it should be pointed out that in two situations different periods of notice apply. First of all, shorter periods of notice apply in the case of bankruptcy (at most six weeks). Moreover, as a result of an amendment of the law in 1999, a special regime applies to employees who were already employed on 1 January 1999 and are 45 years of age or older. For these employees, the regime of terms of notice from before that date applies. These earlier terms involve longer periods of notice.

108. In certain cases, it is not possible to terminate an employment contract.[122] This applies in the following situations:

- an employee who has been ill for less than two years;
- a female employee during pregnancy and subsequent maternity leave;
- a soldier serving as a conscript;

117. Article 7:672, s. 2 Civil Code.
118. Article 7:672, s. 4 Civil Code.
119. Article 7:672, s. 3 Civil Code.
120. Article 7:672, ss 5–7 Civil Code.
121. Article 7:672, s. 9 Civil Code.
122. Article 7:670 Civil Code.

– a member of the works council or staff association;
– refusal to work on Sundays;
– appeal to a statutory leave scheme.

Exceptions have been made in a number of these so-called termination prohibitions – disease under certain conditions, pregnancy and childbirth, military service and workers participation. These prohibitions do not apply, for example, in the cases wherein the employee agrees with the termination, during the probationary period, in case of an instant dismissal or in cases wherein the reason for termination does not relate to the subject of the prohibition.[123]

D. *No Notice or Period of Termination*

109. The law provides for a number of situations in which no period of notice or the requirement of a granted permit or dissolution applies. As an example, parties may agree on a probationary period at the start of the working relationship. The probation period cannot be agreed upon for a fixed-term employment contract with a duration period of six months.

The probation period must be agreed upon in writing. During this period, the employer may dismiss the employee with immediate effect and without giving any reason. In this situation the employer does not need a permit. Because of the severe consequences, the law demands strict requirements for the existence of a legally valid probation clause.[124]Besides the requirement that the clause must be laid down in writing, the probationary period is limited to a maximum amount of time. If this period is exceeded, the entire clause becomes void. According to law, the probation period may be agreed for the length of no more than one month in an employment contract of no more than two years. In an employment contract for a longer period of time or an indefinite period of time the probation period may last a maximum of two months. It should also be pointed out that the term may be extended or reduced in a CLA, in which they may be deviated to the prejudice of an employee.[125]Not only the employer is allowed to terminate the work contract with immediate effect and without giving any reason. The employee can do this as well.[126]

110. Furthermore, when an urgent cause[127] arises, there is a possibility of terminating an employment contract without a dismissal permit and without a term of notice. In such a case, dismissal should happen as soon as the urgent cause arises and the reasons for it should immediately be stated.[128] This procedure is also known as instant dismissal (*ontslag op staande voet*). The law provides for a number of examples that justify instant dismissal, such as severe incompetence or unsuitability

123. Article 7:670a Civil Code.
124. Article 7:602, s. 4 Civil Code.
125. Article 7:652, s. 7 Civil Code.
126. Article 7:676 Civil Code.
127. Consult Arts 7:778 and 7:679 Civil Code.
128. Article 7:677 Civil Code.

of the employee, reckless behaviour, non-compliance with reasonable orders and theft by the employee. Examples justifying instant resignation by the employee are unpaid wages and serious insults. In similar situations, the employment contract comes to an immediate end.

111. The party that invokes the presence of an urgent cause may, if necessary, institute an action based on the violation of the term of notice and/or an action because of manifestly unreasonable dismissal. The employer who is confronted with an employee who wrongfully invokes the presence of an urgent cause may also institute an action based on manifestly unreasonable resignation. The employee who is wrongfully dismissed instantly as a result of the presence of an urgent cause has several options available. First of all, the employee can plead that the employment contract was terminated without a permit to do so. In that case the employment contract continues, if the employer appeals. It is also possible for the employee to claim the applicable period of notice was not applied correctly and/or that the dismissal was manifestly unreasonable.

112. As is seen from case law the existence of an urgent cause is tested severely by the courts. In doing so, the interests of the employer and employee are balanced against each other. The question of whether the gravity of the sanction – instant dismissal – is proportionate is especially taken into consideration by the courts; different sanctions, such as giving a warning or imposing a suspension, are also available as an alternative. In one case, the arbitration board of the Committee of the Royal Dutch Football Association (KNVB) decided that one single act of misconduct of a player on the field could not immediately justify an instant dismissal.[129]

113. The dismissal must be given without delay, at the first real opportunity to do so. Commonly, this is the point in time when the incident arises or is discovered. If necessary, an employee may be suspended under some circumstances, pending the outcome of an inquiry or a decision of the competent authorities (such as a management decision). In general, however, the principle that the dismissal must be given without delay is observed strictly in case law precedents.[130]

114. The employer must prove the urgent cause and that the dismissal was given immediately and the employee has been informed directly. If that is the case, the employee could ask the subdistrict judge to grant him compensation for the wages he could have received during the notice period. The employee may, however, request the subdistrict court to set aside the dismissal for lack of assent. In that case, the employee is entitled to continued payment of wages during the period he did not work due to the termination that has been annihilated by the court.[131] Another possibility is the award of an equitable remuneration by the court.

---

129. Arbitration Tribunal KNVB, 6 Jul. 2001, No. 854, Sportzaken 2001/3 (No. 179) B1 Van Galen/ RBC.
130. Article 7:681 Civil Code.
131. Article 7:670b Civil Code.

E. Termination Agreement

115. The written agreement must be distinguished from the termination agreement. Consent can only be given if the contract is terminated. No notice is required to close a termination agreement. The termination agreement shall only be valid if it is made in writing. The employee has the right to terminate the agreement within fourteen days without giving a reason. If the employer does not mention this option in the termination agreement, the dissolution period will be three weeks. Dissolution can be done only once per six months.

F. Dissolution of an Employment Contract

116. Another possibility of terminating an employment contract unilaterally is upon dissolution of the contract by the court. The request must be based on a reasonable cause (consult paragraph 118).[132]

The termination must be requested by the employer when it comes down to, so-called, personal reasons and can be requested if the UWV has refused to give permission to terminate the employment contract on economic grounds or long-term disability. The employee may request termination if the conditions are such that the employment contract should end immediately or after a short time on the grounds of reasonableness.

The law indicates at which time the employment contract should end by dissolution. The applicable notice period to a minimum of one month is of relevance in this case. In case of serious culpable acts or omissions by the employee the labour contract can be terminated sooner.

In sports law matters, this competence is often granted by regulations of the association to a board of arbitration. To achieve dissolution an employee or employer may present a request to the court.

G. The Revival of the Employment Contract

117. After the termination of the employment contract, the contract can revive in two ways. First by annihilation of the termination, second by recovery of the employment contract.

118. Only the *kantonrechter (subdistrict court)* can annihilate a termination. Annihilation is possible if the employer has terminated in breach of a termination-prohibition, without approval of the employee and without the required approval of the UWV. In the event of an instant dismissal, a breach because of the lack of

132. Article 7:671b Civil Code and Article 7:671c Civil Code.

approval frequently occurs as it relates to personal grounds.[133] An appeal to the annihilation has to be done within two months after the date on which the employment contract ended.[134]

When the termination of the labour contract is annihilated, the labour contract continues as if it has never ended. The employer must continue payment of wages during the period the employee did not work due to the termination. Moderation is possible.

119. Recovery of the labour agreement means that, unlike destruction, the date after which the labour agreement has been recovered is not (always) the same as the date of the end of the contract. Recovery is possible after termination and dissolution. Recovery is in order if the termination of the labour agreement on itself is valid, but does not meet the requirement of a reasonable ground that underlies the termination.[135] The judge may impose the employer to restore the contract and indicates by when it should be done. Even that could lead to a moderation of the wage demand on the side of the employee.[136]

H. Fees

120. Several fees are possible. A fixed fee for the failure to comply with the notice period amounts to the wage that would be due in the correct period of time.[137] This also applies to an instant dismissal where an urgent reason is missing and in case of a temporary contract without the possibility of premature termination.[138] However, it is stated that the Minister of Social Affairs and Employment could establish a higher fee for certain kinds of professions. This has happened to:

- a soccer player who has been registered as a contract player by the KNVB for participating in the men's league of professional football;[139]
- trainer, coach, assistant coach, technical director, technical manager, head of scouting, coordinator of scouting, chief youth trainer and chief specialist trainer, active in professional football.[140]

Reason for this exemption in sports is the transfer system. Usually high fees are paid when a player transfers from one club to another. If the player is essentially free to leave by only paying his salary until the end of the fixed-term contract

133. Article 7:681 Civil Code.
134. Article 7:686a Civil Code.
135. Article 7:682 Civil Code.
136. Article 7:680a Civil Code.
137. Article 7:672, s. 9 Civil Code.
138. Article 7:677, s. 2 Civil Code.
139. Article 7:671b, s.9 Civil Code.
140. Article 7:671c, s. 4 Civil Code and Art. 6:677, s. 6 Civil Code. Consult Regeling ketenbepaling bijzondere functies en hogere vergoeding kantonrechter, *Stcrt.* 2015, 17972.

(which is often much lower than the transfer sum), this transfer system would collapse. Therefore, exemptions have been made for the professional football sector.[141]

121. The second fee is a 'reasonable fee'. The employee is eligible for it if there are any serious culpable acts or omissions on the employer's side and vice versa. The legislator has indicated that a call upon serious culpable acts or omissions is only possible in exceptional cases.

122. In conclusion, the transition compensation. Every employee who is employed is entitled to a transition compensation, if they – apart from a few exceptions – meet the prescribed conditions. The transition compensation is equal to one-third of month's salary per year the employee has been employed by the employer.[142] In case the contract ends in the midst of a year, a compensation pro rata is due. Study costs can be deducted from the transition compensation if it is intended to prevent unemployment or if the period of unemployment is reduced. The costs for wider employability of the employee may also be deducted.[143] The transition compensation is limited to a maximum of EUR 84,000 gross (2021) or an amount equal to the annual salary if the annual salary is higher.[144] In case the contract is terminated on a combination of grounds an additional transition compensation can be granted up to one-half of the original transition compensation.

I. Appeal and Cassation

123. Appeal and cassation can be made against a dissolution granted at the request of the employee, exclusively against compensation awarded by the court and rehabilitation of the labour contract. The end of the labour contract can be determined in appeal and cassation in case of a false rejection of a request for dissolution or if recovery of the employment contract has been wrongly imposed.

J. Systems of Remuneration and/or Transfer Arrangements

124. Systems of remuneration and/or transfer arrangements lack any legal basis in the Netherlands. These are agreements between the employer and the employee/sportsman, in accordance with the regulations of the (international) sports association concerned. The legality must, therefore, be judged, in each case, on the basis of national law. The starting point is when the employee/sportsman has signed approval, the arrangement is, in principle, legitimate. This is no different when the arrangement is based on the regulations of a certain association.

141. S.F.H. Jellinghaus (red.), *Capita Sportrecht,* Antwerpen/'s-Hertogenbosch: Gompel & Scavina 2021, pp. 170–174.
142. Article 7:673, s. 1 and s. 4 Civil Code.
143. Article 7:673, s. 2 Civil Code.
144. Article 7:673, s. 2 Civil Code.

125. The above is seen, for instance, in the so-called *Arnold Mühren* case,[145] in which a football player argued that he was unjustly prohibited from making a transfer from football club FC Twente to AJAX. This transfer was impossible because AJAX, the club that was to take over the player, was unwilling to pay the transfer fee. The player succeeded in his action in every legal instance; nonetheless, the European Commission of Human Rights refused to accept that it was an instance of involuntary servitude, since the player had become a professional of his own free will and, therefore, knew that the transfer system would apply.[146] Under these types of circumstances, each individual situation must be examined to discover whether there has been a violation of national or international legislation, including legislation of the EU. European law is especially important, when the transfer involves nationals of Member States or nationals of associated states. A national who does not fall within these categories cannot, in principle, make an appeal to the regulations of European law.[147]

126. In the Netherlands, a transfer fee can be found particularly in the domain of (professional) football. Partly due to the so-called *Bosman* case,[148] the KNVB has drawn up a regulation that follows the basic ideas of the Federation Internationale de Football Association (FIFA) solidarity system. Dutch law on the termination of employment acts as the starting point for a national transfer of a professional football player. This means that an employment contract for a definite period of time can only be terminated prematurely if the contract contains a clause for premature termination in writing. In the case of premature termination, the party that wishes to terminate owes compensation or ought to have the employment contract dissolved, in the course of which the court may award compensation, in accordance with reasonableness, to the most diligent party. Transfer regulations subsequently state that clubs owe one another reimbursement based on the regulations of their association (solidarity contribution). In addition, these regulations also determine that when an amateur player plays for the first time for a professional football club or concludes an employment contract, reimbursement is due to the clubs that have trained this player.

127. A reimbursement for schooling/training is due when a player under the age of 22 has played in at least five binding matches of the first team of the professional football club or if the player has concluded a player's employment contract. This reimbursement is due to every club where the player has played, from the first year in which he played at least nine matches. For every year of training for the year between the 10th and 20th anniversary of the player, a reimbursement is due by a professional club amounts to EUR 1,523 per year of training.[149] Reimbursement due

145. HR 17 Oct. 1980, NJ 1981, 141.
146. European Commission of Human Rights, 3 May 1983, NJ 1984, 268.
147. Arbitration Tribunal KNVB, 9 Jul. 1996, JAR 1996/192 Kanu.
148. HvJ EG 15 Dec. 1995, ECLI:NL:XX:1995: AD2444.
149. This sum is revised every five years as from 2004.

by amateur football clubs amounts to EUR 562 per year of training. For the years of training before the player turned ten years old, the club receives a one-time payment of the above-mentioned amounts.

128. The clubs pay a solidarity contribution to the clubs at which the player has been registered up to the age of 22 in case of transfer of the player's employment contract from one professional club to another. This contribution encompasses 5% of the reimbursement paid as part of the (premature) termination, as has to be shared by all the previous clubs the player has been trained and educated. To achieve this, the following apportionment formula is applied:

> Article 14 – Calculation of the solidarity contribution 'If a contract player is transferred to another professional football organization during the term of the player's contract, as a solidarity contribution 5 per cent of the reimbursement as referred to in Article 4, paragraph 2 of these regulations, will be divided between the clubs at which the player had been registered as a playing member, in accordance with the following apportionment: Year:
>
> – in which the player has reached the age of 12: 5%;
> – in which the player has reached the age of 13: 5%;
> – in which the player has reached the age of 14: 10%;
> – in which the player has reached the age of 15: 10%;
> – in which the player has reached the age of 16: 10%;
> – in which the player has reached the age of 17: 10%;
> – in which the player has reached the age of 18: 10%;
> – in which the player has reached the age of 19: 10%;
> – in which the player has reached the age of 20: 10%;
> – in which the player has reached the age of 21: 10%;
> – in which the player has reached the age of 22: 10%;
>
> The apportionment takes place in proportion with the number of months a player has been registered as a playing member of the entitled club.'

The reimbursement must be paid by the supplying club to the entitled club within thirty days. If this does not happen, the KNVB guarantees the reimbursement.

V. Transfer of Undertakings

129. As a result of European regulations and based on all of the relevant facts and circumstances, freedom of contract is breached in the case of the passing of ownership of an undertaking.[150] When this situation arises, all rights and obligations that apply to the employer with regard to the employee, at the time of the passing transfer over to the acquiring party by operation of law, under the same employment conditions as before, including acquired seniority. Therefore, for this

150. Article 7:662 Civil Code.

purpose, consensus is not required. The same applies in principle to pension obligations[151] and obligations ensuing from the applicable (mandatory) CLA.[152] These regulations do not apply to the crews of seagoing vessels or to (in general) employers in a state of bankruptcy.[153]

VI. Collective Dismissal and Closure of Enterprises

130. Based on European regulations, Dutch law provides for a special procedure meant for collective dismissal (the Collective Redundancy Notification Act; Wet melding collectief ontslag (WMCO)). This applies when an employer intends to dismiss twenty or more employees within one field of activity within a period of three months. When these regulations apply, the employer is obliged to report the intended dismissal to the UWV as well as to the representative collective industrial organizations. This involves particularly those organizations that have members within the company. The purpose of this notification is so consultation with the trade unions concerning the collective dismissals can take place and so that a 'Social plan' may be arranged to ease the consequences for the employees. Among other things, the notification must contain as much information as possible about the following matter:

- the considerations leading to the intended decision;
- the number of employees involved, assigned to occupation/function, age and sex;
- the total number of employees;
- the points in time at which the employment relationship ought to come to an end;
- the criteria used to decide on the dismissal of these employees;
- the possible redundancy scheme; and
- the position of the existing works council, if any.

131. After notification to the UWV, the consideration of the dismissal is postponed for one month in order to give the management and trade unions time to discuss the matter. Subsequently the consideration is continued in a normal manner (regardless of the result of the discussions). The term of one month may be shortened by means of an agreement with the trade union or in case of an urgent situation as a result of which the employment of more employees is at stake. Failure to comply with the obligations arising from this law results in the postponement by the UWV of all pending dismissal proceedings for a period of two months. It should be pointed out that in these situations the works council also plays a part. A collective dismissal will often coincide with a reorganization, which must be presented to the works council for advice. Furthermore, many CLAs contain special provisions applicable to this subject.

151. Article 7:664 Civil Code.
152. Article 14A WCA (Collective Labour Agreements Act), 2A WAVV.
153. Article 7:666 Civil Code.

§4. LABOUR MARKET REGULATION

I. Employment of Foreign Workers

132. Employment of foreign workers is regulated in different laws and treaties:

- Law on employing aliens (Wav), which stipulates when a working permit is necessary.
- Rome I- Regulation, which is decisive on which law is applicable on the labour agreement with the foreign worker.
- Sham Employment Arrangements Act (WAS), which provides payment of minimum wage in specific circumstances.
- Law on labour conditions of posted workers within the EU (WagwEU); which stipulates the labour conditions of foreign employees posted in the Netherlands.
- EEX-Regulation II, stipulates which court is competent in international disputes.

133. There are two groups of foreign workers: EU nationals and non-EU nationals. EU nationals can work freely in the whole area of the EU. This is the freedom of movement. Since 1 May 2007, nationals from the new Member States (Poland, Slovakia, Hungary, Czech Republic, Slovenia, Estonia, Latvia and Lithuania) and Croatia as of 2013, can also work freely in the Netherlands. Before this date, they had to apply for a work permit. Non-EU nationals are not allowed to perform labour without a work permit in the Netherlands.[154] The work permit has to be applied by the employer (according to Article 6 WAV) and the permit can be awarded for a maximum period of one year (according to Article 11 WAV). This permit has to be obtained from the UWV or, if the intended working period is longer than three months the Integration and Naturalization Agency (IND). If a group of employees is exempted by a general regulation, it is not necessary to apply for a work permit. This also applies to foreigners with unconditional residence permits (*see* Article 4, Foreign Nationals Employment Act). Foreign employees having permanent residence in the Netherlands for over five years on the basis of a residence permit do not have to apply for a work permit.

134. The intended employer has to apply for the work permit, according to Article 6 WAV. The UWV is under an obligation to settle the application within five weeks after the application. The UWV has to reject the permit if:[155]

- there is a sufficient labour force on the Dutch labour market in respect to the employment opportunity concerned;
- the registration at UWV of the employment opportunity has not been made at least five weeks before the application for the work permit;
- the foreigner does not have a legitimate title for his stay or did not request one;
- to whom a permit has been refused of whose permit has been revoked;
- the foreigner does not earn at least the minimum wage with the intended labour;

154. Article 1, Foreign Nationals Employment Act (Wet arbeid vreemdelingen (WAV)).
155. Article 8, Foreign Nationals Employment Act.

- it is prescribed by general rule that the intended labour is not allowed to be performed by foreigners considering the national interest;
- the employer cannot demonstrate that he has made sufficient effort to fill the vacancy in the Dutch labour market;
- in case of a certain category of work or foreigners for which in accordance with Article 5, a limited number of permits is permitted, which limit has been reached.

The Minister may possibly deviate from these grounds for refusal in special circumstances or the freezing of commercial relations or in the context of the performance of spiritual, religious or philosophical functions and in the case of education, volunteer work, training or international exchange and international cultural contacts.

135. Beside the reasons listed above, the Minister can reject the permit if:[156]

(1) the vacancy is expected to be filled by the Dutch labour market within a reasonable period of time;
(2) the employee is beyond the scope of the determined age limits;
(3) the requirements for a previous permit have not been met;
(4) no suitable accommodation is available for the foreigner;
(5) the employer is no recognized referent as referred to in Article 1, part t of the Aliens Act 2000, because his approval is revoked or suspended, or because his application for recognition was rejected;
(6) the employer is a referent as referred to in Article 1, part s of the Aliens Act 2000, or a recognized referent as referred to in Article 1, part t of that Act and who have had an administrative fine on the grounds of Article 55a of that Act or has been sanctioned on the ground of Article 108 of that Act in the five years prior to the application for a work permit or a combined permit;
(7) in a period of five years prior to the application for a permit or a combined permit an administrative fine has been imposed on the employer based on:
    - Article 10:1 of the Working Hours Act (Arbeidstijdenwet).
    - Article 33 of the Working Conditions Act (Arbeidsomstandighedenwet).
    - Article 18b of the Minimum Wage and Minimum Holiday Allowance Act (Wet minimumloon en minimumvakantiebijslag).
    - Article 18 of the Aliens Act (Wet arbeid vreemdelingen).
    - Article 16 of the Allocation of Workers by Intermediaries Act (Wet allocatie arbeidskrachten door intermediars).
(8) the employer has been punished in a period of five years prior to the application for a permit or a combined permit based on:
    - Article 273f of the Dutch Criminal Code (Wetboek van strafrecht).
    - Article 11:3 of the Working Hours Act (Arbeidstijdenwet).
    - Article 32 of the Working Conditions Act (Arbeidsomstandighedenwet).
(9) the employer has put obstacles in the way as a result of which the vacancy cannot be filled by the Dutch labour market;

156. Article 9, Foreign Nationals Employment Act.

(10) when the recruitment has not been carried out in a way that has been agreed on by the relevant sector in a covenant that meets the requirements set up by a ministerial arrangement (according to Article 9 term 1 sub eWAV). The requirements of the covenant have been laid down in term 2 of Article 9 WAV.

The requirements for the ministerial arrangement, meant in the first term under h, contain at least the following:

– The Institute on Social securities (Uitvoeringsinstituut werknemers verzekeringen) is one of the parties in the covenant. They have to inform the Minister of Social Matters and Employment about the intention to set up the covenant. And the covenant should be published in 'de Staatscourant' when it has been worked out.

136. The work permit will be granted for a period of one year at most, in which case it is possible that a non-extension can be issued in advance. In the case of temporary labour, the permit will in principle be granted for a period of twenty-four weeks at most the minister of Justice and Safety, may connect to rules to permits or combined permits to ensure that:[157]

– the effort to be made by the employer to fill the vacancy by the Dutch labour market;
– the differences to be removed regarding the terms of employment, labour relations and working conditions;
– that the labour contract will be made in writing and that a copy will be made available to the authority which provides the permit;
– the provision of sufficient training and education within the labour organization by the employer.

137. The Minister may revoke a permit if, during the application, false or incomplete information has been supplied. In addition, the work permit can be withdrawn if the residence permit is not granted or the permit has not been used. Finally, the permit can be withdrawn if the requirements of the permit have not been met. After the grant of the permit, the employer has to keep a copy of the identification papers of the employee for a period of five years after the termination of the working relationship. The employee/foreigner is under an obligation to give the employer the opportunity to make a copy of his identification papers. In the case of transfer of the employee/foreigner to a recipient, the employer has to ensure that the recipient receives a copy of the work permit.

The Minister of Justice and Safety can revoke a combined permit if:

– the employer is not a recognized referent as referred to in Article 1, part t of the Aliens Act 2000, because his approval is revoked or suspended, or because his application for recognition was rejected;

157. Article 10, Foreign Nationals Employment Act.

- the employer is a referent as referred to in Article 1, part s of the Aliens Act 2000, or a recognized referent as referred to in Article 1, part t of that Act and who have had an administrative fine on the grounds of Article 55a of that Act or has been sanctioned on the ground of Article 108 of that Act in the five years prior to the application for a work permit or a combined permit;
- if the permit is a combined permit, the withdrawal grounds provided for in Article 19 of the Aliens Act 2000 regarding a permit for a fixed period as mentioned in Article 14 of the Aliens Act will also apply.

The Minister or the Minister of Security and Justice can also revoke a combined permit if in a period of five years prior to the application for a permit or a combined permit:

(1) an administrative fine CAN has been imposed on the employee based on:
   (a) Article 10:1 of the Working Hours Act (Arbeidstijdenwet).
   (b) Article 33 of the Working Conditions Act (Arbeidsomstandighedenwet).
   (c) Article 18b of the Minimum Wage and Minimum Holiday Allowance Act (Wet minimumloon en minimumvakantiebijslag).
   (d) Article 18b of the Minimum Wage and Minimum Holiday Allowance Act (Wet minimumloon en minimumvakantiebijslag).
   (e) Article 16 of the Allocation of Workers by Intermediaries Act (Wet allocatie arbeidskrachten door intermediars).
(2) an employee can be punished based on:
   (a) Article 273f of the Dutch Criminal Code (Wetboek van strafrecht).
   (b) Article 11:3 of the Working Hours Act (Arbeidstijdenwet).
   (c) Article 32 of the Working Conditions Act (Arbeidsomstandighedenwet).

138. A possible fine guarantees the compliance of these statutory obligations. According to Article 23, part 1 of the Foreign Nationals Employment Act, the employer is obliged to pay the salaries of the employees who performed labour as mentioned in Article 2, part J of Directive nr. 2009/52/EG providing for minimum standards on sanctions and measures against employers of illegally staying third-country nationals. The foreigner can hold all next higher employers liable for the fulfilment of Article 23 part 1 Foreign Nationals Employment Act. An employee could set up a claim under part 3 of the article if the claim to the nearest lower employer has failed. The subdistrict court judge is competent to review the claims. These regulations have a considerable effect on the sports world. A distinction has to be made, however, between taking part in sporting competitions, a work placement/test training, and actually being employed.

139. A foreigner who has his principal place of residence outside the Netherlands and occasionally takes part in sporting competitions in the Netherlands or is working as a permanent personal coach of a participant in sports competitions, for example, in an international tournament, is not under an obligation to apply for a work permit as long as the competition concerned does not last longer than six weeks within a period of thirteen weeks.[158] The rules change if it is a matter of a work placement or training. Viewed separately, a work placement is not covered by these regulations as long as it is a 'clear' work placement, that is to say, with a connection to the education of the person concerned. The educational establishment involved is under an obligation to make a statement with respect to that. However, in the sports branch, this situation usually will not apply.

140. In consultation with organized employees in the football branch, specific criteria have been laid down. If the professional football player meets these criteria, a work permit can be granted. A work permit for professional sportsmen will in general be rejected:

– when it concerns a job in a lower division than the highest division of the concerning sports association; and/or
– if the remuneration is not in accordance with what is usually paid, the value of the usual transfer sum must be deducted from the remuneration. Remuneration that is not in accordance with usual payment will normally occur when the remuneration is lower than the usual remuneration of players who belong to the top 20% in the highest league of the concerning branch of sport; or
– it concerns a player who has not directly, before the employment, taken part on a regular basis in a competition that is at least qualitative equivalent to the highest division in the Netherlands (top forty FIFA-ranking) or who has not in another way, like taking part in the World/European (youth) Championship, the Olympic games or the Champions/Europe League, shown to have at least equivalent qualities. This is called the quality criterion.

II. Employment Intermediation and Player Agents

141. The regulations concerning employment intermediation and player agents, the Placement of Personnel by Intermediaries Act (*Wet allocatie arbeidskrachten door intermediairs* (WAADI) of 1 May 1998 have recently been amended (2021).[159]

142. The KNVB introduced regulations on 1 April 2015 in regard to players' agents. The so-called Intermediaries Regulation is intended to regulate the intermediaries in the interest of Dutch football. Only those persons who are registered at the KNVB as an intermediate may act as such. The introduction is a direct result of

158. *See* Art. 1, para. 1 sub (a) and (6), Decree on the implementation of the Foreign Nationals Employment Act.
159. *See* on this matter: M.K.W. van den Berg & S.F.H. Jellinghaus, '*Voetbalmakelaars in de Nederlandse sport*', in *Transfer En Makelaars in De Sport*, ed. F. Hendricks (Intersentia, 2002) and S.F.H. Jellinghaus, '*The Netherlands*', in *C.S. Playersagents Worldwide*, ed. R. Siekmann (D.M.C. Asser Press, 2007); *see also* J. van Drongelen, '*Over spelersmakelaars en andere belangenbehartigers in de voetbalwereld*', TvS&R 2011–2012, 49–54.

the FIFA decision to abolish the licensing system for players' agents. The FIFA Congress adopted amendments to the FIFA Statutes on 11 June 2014 allowing players' agents and fiduciaries to no longer have to pass an exam in order to act as an intermediary.

However, they must be registered with a Football Association to be allowed to be involved in a transaction. FIFA now uses a 'minimum program' for intermediaries, but offers all the national football associations the room to expand it. This resulted in the KNVB's 'Intermediaries Regulation'. In order to be registered as an intermediate at KNVB, intermediaries must sign an intermediate declaration and present the following documents:

– A completed and signed intermediary declaration.
– A copy of a valid passport and/or valid identity card.
– An original Statement of Conduct.

From 1 April 2015, the KNVB keeps a register of intermediaries and publishes it on its website. The registration is valid for a maximum of one year. Every year, on 31 March, the names of all registered intermediaries and the transactions with Dutch clubs in which they were involved are published.

Registered intermediaries are bound by the statutes and/or regulations of the KNVB, Union of European Football Associations (UEFA) and/or FIFA and/or decisions of one or more of their organs and under the jurisdiction of the organs of the KNVB, including the disciplinary bodies and the college of arbitrators.

The KNVB is developing a certification system for organizations which work with intermediaries. In this way, the KNVB wants to ensure the quality of players' agents who are members of certified organizations.

For more information about FIFA regulations on intermediaries *see* the publication by Wil Van Megen and Dennis Koolaard.[160]

III. Placing Sportsmen at the Disposal of Users

143. A sportsman (amateur or professional) can be sponsored, but both the sportsman and the sponsor must realize that under certain circumstances the sponsorship may be viewed as an employment contract. To prevent this, the sponsorship (money or otherwise) must not be considered salary. This definition of sponsorship is interpreted broadly by legislation. In addition, the services from the sportsman have to be of such a nature that there is no subordinate relationship. Furthermore, reference should be made to what has been mentioned above concerning flexible employment relations (*see* Chapter 2, §1, III, C).

160. www.sportslawbulletin.com.

§5. SOCIAL SECURITY

144. Dutch social security laws can be characterized as complicated. This chapter seeks to describe in broad outline the relevant regulations. The system roughly consists of two types of regulations, namely national insurance schemes and employed persons' insurance schemes. National insurance schemes are facilities applying, in principle, to every inhabitant of the Netherlands. Examples of this are the Participation Act (Participatiewet) and the General Old Age Pensions Act (AOW). Funding of these schemes is achieved through the levying of taxes. In principle, employed persons' insurance schemes apply to employees only. A certain percentage of their wages is deducted as a contribution. Examples of these schemes are the Unemployment Insurance Act and the Disablement Benefits Act (WW/WIA).

145. The management of the employed persons' insurance scheme is assigned to the body implementing employee insurance schemes, called UWV. This involves both the recovery of the premiums due as well as the attribution and disbursement of benefits. According to Chapter 13 of the Social Insurance Funding Act, the concept of 'wages' over which social insurance contributions must be paid is given a broad interpretation. According to Article 16 of the act this involves 'all that which is earned from employment'. There are only a few exceptions to this, for example, the pension scheme.

146. Dutch social security law contains a special provision for professional sportsmen. This provision can be found in Article 4a of the so-called Curiosity Royal Decree.[161] According to this decree a sportsman practising a certain sport as a profession is considered to be an employee for the purposes of social security legislation. Furthermore, the regulation states that the relationship in which the employee enjoys a periodical compensation for living expenses in accordance with the decreed code on the part of the Ministry of Health, Welfare and Sports and the Professional Sportsmen Fund is considered to be an employer/employee relationship. This applies to sportsmen with a so-called A or B status. Since 1 January 2001, this involves especially those sportsmen who receive a grant to cover their living expenses in order to devote themselves completely to the practice of top-class sport. This grant arrangement involves a monthly contribution of a maximum of 70% of the statutory minimum wage plus an allowance for expenses for a top-class sportsman with A-status; an income limit applies. Receiving this grant, the sportsman commits himself to do everything possible to retain his A-status. By means of this regulation insurance, in the sense of social security, is achieved for top-class sportsmen.

According to Article 1 term 2 of the decree this employment falls under the Dutch social security law.

Article 4a applies to Athletes with an A-, B- or HP-status.

161. Royal Decree of 24 Dec. 1986, stb. 1986, 655.

I. Work Incapacity

A. *Illness*

147. In case of illness, the employee is not obliged to work. For the first 104 weeks (two years) of the illness the employer is obliged to continue paying the employee's wages.[162] This obligation applies only to 70% of the wages, limited by the so-called maximum daily pay.[163] Furthermore, the salary during illness may not amount to less than minimum wage. In practice, in many cases, payment of 100% of the wages is continued because of arrangements in CLAs. In the CLA Sports a provision is included which provides employees with 100% of their wages during the first year of work incapacity if they fulfil their obligations with regards to their reintegration. After these 104 weeks, the employment contract with the employer continues, but the employer is no longer obliged to pay wages. In that case, if the employee is still ill, he will have to have recourse to an occupational disability benefit and/or an unemployment benefit. Recently the Supreme Court decided that an employer is obliged to terminate the contract after 104 weeks, if the only reason he is not terminating is to avoid paying the Transition Payment.[164]

148. Furthermore, it is possible to agree in the employment contract that the first two days of illness will not be paid for. In conclusion, it should be pointed out that several insurance companies insure the risk entailed by the obligation to continue payment of wages in the event of illness. The extent of the insurance premium depends mostly on the absence through illness. An employment contract with the employee cannot be terminated because of illness, unless the employee has been ill for more than two years and recovery is not to be expected within six months.[165] However, the approval of the UWV Werkbedrijf is still required. In the Netherlands, every employer is obliged to be associated with a working conditions service. This service is to support the employer during the illness of an employee, and its goal is for the employee to be reintegrated into employment as soon as possible, whether or not on a therapeutic basis.

149. Reintegration, as provided for by the so-called *Wet Verbetering Poortwachter*, is of grave importance. According to this act, the employer must engage actively in the reintegration of an employee during his illness. In effect this involves the following:

- A report of illness must be passed on to the working conditions service, on the very first day of illness.
- The employer must keep a record, with the working conditions service, concerning the course of the inability to work and the reintegration of the employee.

162. Article 7:629 Civil Code.
163. EUR 223,40 a day as from 1 Jan. 2021.
164. HR 8 Nov. 2019, ECLI:NL:HR:2019:1734.
165. Article 7:670 Civil Code and Art. 7 UWV agreement dismissal procedure (Regeling UWV ontslagprocedure).

- Within six weeks from the first day of illness the employer must have a reintegration plan drafted by the working conditions service. If it is apparent from this plan that the return of the employee is a possibility, the employer must, within two weeks thereafter, draft a plan of approach in which it is shown how the reintegration will be carried out, in agreement with the employee.
- Within forty-two weeks the disability to work must be reported to the UWV. If the employer fails to give this notice within forty-two weeks, he will be fined.
- After fifty-two weeks the employer and employee draw up, together, an evaluation of the first year. This contains a statement of the progress in the reintegration.
- In the seventeenth month following the first day of illness, the employee receives a letter from the UWV. In this letter the UWV indicates the possibility of claiming a disability benefit for the period following the continued payment of the employer.
- Two weeks before, after ninety weeks, the employee files an application for the allowance of a disability benefit, the employer, in agreement with the employee, must draft a reintegration report. The employee must also receive a copy of this report.

The employer is not obliged to inform the UWV when the employee recovers from his illness. The report must contain data on the company, the position of the employee, the plan of approach, the most recent evaluation of the plan of approach, the planned reintegration activities, an assessment of the quality of the working relationship, the limitations and the possibilities of the employee and the availability of suitable work. Furthermore, the employee must be given the opportunity to comment on every aspect. In a diagram format, the course of illness can be displayed as follows:

First day of illness	*Report of illness passed on to UWV*
6 weeks	Reintegration advice
8 weeks	Plan of approach for possible return
42 weeks	Informing the UWV about the
	disability to work
52 weeks	First-year evaluation including a
	statement of the reintegration process.
17 months	Receiving application for a disability
	benefit (before the end of the period of
	illness of two years)
24 months	End of the obligation of the employer
	to continue payment of wages.

Twenty-four months of protection against dismissal ends. After that: either the Unemployment Act (WW) or the Income and Ability to Work Act (WIA) can be applied for. In case the employer has not fulfilled his duties in regard to the above-mentioned obligations, he can be sanctioned with a so-called 'loon sanctie', which means the period that the employer must pay wages is extended with a maximum of fifty-two weeks (one year).

150. The possibility exists that the employer may dispute the illness of the employee. There may also be discussion about whether the employee has been offered suitable alternative work, considering his limitations. In that case, the employer has the right to defer the continued payment of wages. Subsequently, the employee may institute an action to recover his/her wages. Nevertheless, this can only happen if the employee has previously obtained a so-called professional review from the UWV (or if the employer and the working conditions service of the employer disagree). In this professional review, an independent UWV physician gives his opinion on the matter. If this physician declares that he considers the employee fit for work, the employee is entitled to a bridging benefit until the court has eventually passed judgment on the action to recover his/her wages. For the record, it should be pointed out that the court is not bound by the judgment of the UWV physician and/or of the working conditions service. In practice, in such cases, the employer uses the method of instant dismissal because it is a matter of refusal to work. This approach, however, is a dangerous one, especially since the courts are not inclined to accept such a dismissal because of the serious implications for the employee. Furthermore, it is possible for an employee to request a second opinion from a different doctor. This is a different procedure than the above mentioned, because this second opinion is not executed by UWV and does not have to be paid for by the employee.

B. Disability

151. In section 144 it is pointed out that during the period of illness the employer is, in principle, under the obligation to continue payment of 70% of the wages of the employee. After a period of 104 weeks the employee may possibly be entitled to invalidity benefits. This is laid down in the WIA.

The aim of the WIA is to increase the productivity of the working population and to limit the intake of persons who are incapable of work. The main reference of this law is the earning capacity of the employee, which is what the employee still earns with his restrictions. The WIA consists of two regulations:

(1) Persons Wholly Unfit for Work Income Scheme (IVA).
(2) Persons Partially Unfit for Work Resumption of Work Scheme (WGA).

152. In regard to earning capacity, a clear distinction must be made between 'to be sick' and 'to be incapable of working'. Sickness can lead to incapacity for work. If an employee becomes incapable of work, medical testing will be put in place to evaluate what exactly are the employee's physical restrictions. Additionally, an employment expert will review what kind of labour the employee, with his physical restrictions, can still perform (employment expert testing) and what income can be generated. For this purpose, it is not important if there is a concrete job opening for this new job function. For example, a painter can perform secretarial duties despite his physical limitations. The employee earned in his old job function as a painter the same wage as in his new function as a secretary. In that case, the employee's capacity to work is 100%, the incapacity to work zero. If he should only earn half the amount of wages in the new job function, then the incapacity to work is 50%. This testing takes place by means of the criteria mentioned in the so-called Estimate Decision (*Schattingsbesluit*).

153. After two years of illness, insurance doctors and labour experts of the UWV assess which work the employee is still capable of performing. As a result of the Eligibility for Permanent Invalidity Benefit Restrictions Act (Wvp), employers have been given greater responsibility for the reintegration of their employees (active reintegration obligation employer). As a result of the WIA, after two years of continuous payment of 70% of the employee's last-earned salary, the employer has to fulfil more and more reintegration obligations. In this context, the employees themselves will also have a greater responsibility. The WIA provides financial incentives to promote the resumption of work. In principle, the WIA is carried out by UWV. The employer can choose to bear the risk of paying the invalidity benefit herself or obtain insurance to cover the risk.

Within the WIA, four possibilities exist:

(1) the employee is incapacitated less than 35%;
(2) the employee is partially incapable of work (35%–80%);
(3) the employee is partially incapable of work for at least 80% or more;
(4) the employee is permanently and entirely unable to work.

If the employee is entirely unable to work and there is no, or hardly any, chance the situation will improve, the employee will be assessed as suffering 'complete and durable incapacity for work'. In that case the employee has a right to a benefit based on the IVA. The IVA is carried out by UWV.

The employee who can partially perform activities can be considered as 'partial labour-suitable'. This employee falls under the regulation of the WGA.

154. When it is established that an employee is less than 35% incapable of work, he is considered to continue in the labour process. The employee is, therefore, considered capable of performing activities; these will not necessarily be his own (former) activities. The employee receives no benefits and stays on the payroll of the employer. The employer must re-integrate this employee within or outside the company. The employer must search for appropriate labour or he has to continue the reintegration route. Under Article 7:611 BW the employer has the duty to adapt the workplace to the employee's disability. If the reintegration does not succeed, the employee can turn to social security benefits: Participation Act, WW or Act on Income Provisions for Older or Partially Disabled, Formerly Unemployed Persons (IOAW)-benefit.

Because of the fact that the dismissal prohibition due to sickness no longer exists when the period of two years has expired, the employer has the possibility to apply for a dismissal licence at the UWV Werkbedrijf. The reason for dismissal in this case is the misfunctioning of the employee. The UWV Werkbedrijf will obtain recommendations of the UWV and will then decide if the employee can or cannot re-integrate at the employer's enterprise.

155. If an employee is more than 35%, but less than 80% incapable of work, he is considered to be able to perform 'partial activities'. In that case the employee receives a wage-related WGA-benefit. The duration of this benefit is a minimum of three months and a maximum of twenty-four months, depending on the employment history of the employee before he became sick.

To determine the employment history, the calendar years from 1998 until the calendar year before the first day of sickness will be examined. In any case, the employee must have worked a minimum of twenty-six of the last thirty-six weeks before he became sick.

The WGA-benefit is 70% of the difference between the last-earned wages and the possible income that still could be earned. If the employee does not work, then the amount of the benefit is 70% of the last-earned wages (up to the maximum daily wage). When employee is fully incapable of working, but their incapability is not of a permanent nature, they receive a WGA-benefit. The amount of this benefit is the same as an IVA-benefit. The employee who falls under the WGA regulation has a right to reintegration conciliation of the UWV.

The duration of the WIA benefit is equal to the duration of the WW benefit.

Employment History	*WIA*
6 months	2 months 75% + 1 month 70%
4 years	4 months 70%
5 years	5 months
10 years	10 months
15 years	12,5 months
20 years	15 months
25 years	17.5 months
30 years	20 months
35 years	22.5 months
38 years	24 months
40 years	24 months

As mentioned before, as of 1 January 2016, the maximum duration of the WGA benefit will be shortened by one month for each passing quarter up to a new maximum of twenty-four months. In some cases, employees may be entitled to an extra-long duration based on a CLA.

156. After a WGA wage-related benefit, the employee receives a wage supplement, under the condition that he earns more than half of his remaining earning capacity. If the employee earns less than half, then he receives a continuation benefit. A wage supplement gives the right to a benefit of 75% for the first two months, after that 70% per month of the difference between the daily wage and the remaining earning capacity. A wage supplement is always higher than a continuation benefit. Also, in this case, the employer must provide suitable work for the employee.

157. An employee who is partially suitable to perform work, but does not work or who earns less than half of what he could earn, because of his labour restriction, is entitled to a continuation benefit of 70% of the minimum wage, multiplied by the rate of incapacity. A working employee who earns at least half of his remaining earning capacity receives, as mentioned above, a wage supplement of 75% of the difference between the old remuneration and the remaining earning capacity. Up to age 65 and 66 as of 2018 and 67 as of 2021, the partial labour-suitable employee is in principle entitled to either a continuation benefit or a wage supplement.

158. Only an employee who is completely and durably incapable of work qualifies for a benefit under the IVA regulation. Complete incapacity for work is present when there are no possibilities of earning, for example, persons who have been committed to an institution, persons who are bedridden, persons who are physically not independent and persons with a serious mental impairment with incapacity to personally and socially function. Persons who still have possibilities to perform work, but with a remuneration loss of 80% or more, are also considered entirely incapable of work.

If an employee is entirely incapable of work and there is no chance that the situation will improve, resumption of work is generally impossible. In that case the employee is entitled to an IVA-benefit of at least 75% from the last-earned wages to the maximum day wage (maximum day wage amounts to EUR 223,40 in 2021). If the employee does not stay in a nursing home, but does stay in a permanent condition that requires permanent care, the invalidity benefit will be raised for the period of the permanent care with a maximum factor of 100/75.

In principle, the IVA-benefit has an indefinite duration. An employee who is entirely incapable of work, but has a small chance of recuperation, receives a benefit of 75% of his last-earned wages. This benefit is not based on the worker's employment history.

According to the above, a considerably long route has to be travelled before the employee qualifies for an IVA-benefit. But if the employee does qualify for an IVA-benefit, he enjoys a guarantee of reasonable income.

Seventy per cent of possible income from labour will be diminished from the IVA-benefit; this means that 30% is released. Furthermore, for people who, before they got disabled, earned more than the maximum daily income, a correction takes place to avert the situation in which they would not receive a benefit because they earned more than the maximum daily income, while the income is still significantly lower than the income they received before they got disabled.

159. During a period of five years, the employee is retested annually to see if there has been any improvement. During these tests the possibilities of the employee resuming work are investigated. The right to an IVA-benefit exists as long as the incapacity for work continues. If the employee succeeds in earning 20% of his original wage or more, a discount will be taken off of his benefit in the first place. If this situation continues for more than two years, the employee is no longer considered to be completely and durably incapable of work. In that case, the employee will receive a transfer from an IVA-benefit to a WGA-benefit. The CBBS-System is used to find appropriate functions for the employee which they still can perform and which are available.

160. For the part of salary for which there is no right to disability benefits, the employee may apply for unemployment benefits. In that case, the employee will have to meet all requirements with respect to receiving unemployment benefits, as mentioned above. It is common knowledge that the performance of any sportsman declines as he grows older. This fact is also taken into consideration in determining the disability percentage received by the sportsman. In the case of a (semi-) professional football player, for instance, is it assumed that when he reaches the age of 35, he will have to change to a different job.[166]

II. Unemployment

161. In case of unemployment, the employee may be entitled to unemployment benefits. Unemployment means that an employee has lost at least five, or half, of his working hours a week and is available to work. As a starting point for calculating the number of working hours lost, use the average number of working hours over the last twenty-six weeks preceding the loss of working hours is used. Subsequently, to obtain an entitlement to the benefit, the employee must have worked as an employee for at least twenty-six weeks out of the thirty-six weeks preceding the unemployment and, furthermore, in the last five years he must at least have earned wages for 208 hours per year or have received unemployment benefits for this period. This is required because, to establish a right to a long-term unemployment benefit, a strong link with the labour process is expected. Because of the above-mentioned definition, it is not necessary for entitlement to an unemployment benefit to be fully dismissed. In addition, it is also possible an employee will receive unemployment benefits in the case of frost, snow, high water or other extraordinary weather conditions. No entitlement to a benefit exists, when the employee is entitled to another benefit, for instance, because of disability or unemployment as a result of a strike or if the employee is not staying in the Netherlands or is in detention. In case the employer has to pay wages but refuses, there is no right to benefits. In that case the employee has to force his employer to pay, because this is not considered unemployment.

166. CRvB, RSV 1976, 105 and USZ 1997, 239. An older age applies to goalkeepers; *see* CRvB 17 Jun. 1998, USZ 1998, 213.

162. If the employee meets the requirements, he is entitled to a benefit in the amount of 75% of his last-earned wages with the 'maximum daily pay' as a maximum for the first two months of unemployment.[167] The duration of the benefit amounts to:

Employment History	*WW*
6 months	2 months 75% + 1 month 70%
4 years	4 months 70%
5 years	5 months
10 years	10 months
15 years	12.5 months
20 years	15 months
25 years	17.5 months
30 years	20 months
35 years	22.5 months
38 years	24 months
40 years	24 months

The employment history is calculated using the days actually worked in the past five years and the years between the employee's 18th birthday until 1998. As from 1998, the genuinely worked years are taken into account. As of 1998 until 2012, each calendar year wherein the employee has earned wages over at least fifty-two days will be taken into account when calculating the maximum duration of employment benefits. When the employee is likely to drop below the guaranteed minimum income with his benefit, he can receive a supplement up to the social minimum income, based on the Supplementary Benefits Act.

After the expiry of the unemployment benefit, the employee may appeal to the assistance benefit from his municipality to the extent of the guaranteed minimum. People born before 1 January 1965 and with insufficient income to provide their daily needs qualify for the benefit based on the IOAW:

- The person who got dismissed after reaching the age of 50, in accordance with his unemployment, was entitled to receive an unemployment benefit under 'hoofdstuk II' of the WW for the length of more than three months, and subsequently receives the full benefit length, meant in 'Hoofdstuk II of the Unemployment Act', a possible extension included.
- The person who, after reaching the age of 50, is entitled to a WGA-benefit as meant in 'Hoofdstuk 7' of the WIA Act, and his right to this benefit has been ended because his level of work unsuitability is no longer at least 35%.

167. EUR 223,40 a Day of January 2021.

This benefit is at guaranteed minimum income level too, on the condition that in that case a review of income and wealth applies. This means that the employee's entire financial situation is taken into account. Furthermore, an employee is obliged to try and avoid becoming unemployed and/or remaining unemployed as much as possible from the time he knows he is becoming unemployed. This means, for instance, that he must try to find suitable employment (make-work applications) and should accept suitable employment.[168] If the employee does not comply with this, UWV may impose a sanction that may amount to a complete denial of the benefits. Moreover, it is worth mentioning that for other employees (40 years of age or over) the accrual of former pension rights is continued after dismissal, after a waiting period of 180 days, for the length of the unemployment benefit.

III. Pensions

163. Dutch law does not recognize a general claim to pensions for employees, other than social benefits for everyone above 67 (AOW). In addition private pension can be built up and should be mutually agreed on by employee and employer. Mostly this has been settled by (mandatory) CLAs. In addition, Dutch law provides several safeguards. Insurance companies and pension funds must inform their participants, at least once a year, about their pensions. For instance, a pension must, in principle, be (formally) built up outside the company. This may be achieved by placing it with an insurance company or with a self-administered pension scheme. A self-administered pension scheme usually takes the form of a foundation in which the pensions for a company or business sector are build up. For this accrual of pension rights, specific legal provisions apply to provide for a sound and sensible accrual of pension rights. The Dutch Central Bank (DNB) is in charge of the supervision in this respect. Employees from 21 years of age must be able to participate in a pension scheme. Within the branch of sports, there are several specific pension funds. The most well-known of these is the fund established on behalf of professional football players and professional cyclists, the so-called Contract Players Fund (CFK). This fund can make use of a tax facility, through which professional football players may add money to the fund in a tax-friendly manner in order to provide for them after their active football career is over. Furthermore, the fund provides for a dependent's pension and a provision for old age. The fund also advises football players on their financial planning.

A. Fundraising

164. The foundation obtains its income by money football clubs are obliged to pay, by return on investments, and from everything acquired by bequest and endowment. Article 1 paragraph 2 of the Pension Scheme Rules and Regulations states that the employment contract between a professional football player and his club must contain a provision under which the club grants the player a pension right. Every

168. Article 24 WW.

player's contract, therefore, must contain a provision in which the percentage of the wages that is to be added to the pension fund is described. The Pension Scheme Rules and Regulations contain a schedule in Article 5 in which the amount that is to be added in view of the allowance is laid down. All payments the professional player is entitled to receive are considered allowance, including match premiums and expenses for international matches. However, holiday allowances and reimbursement of expenses are excluded.

B. Pensions and Benefits

165. The starting point for the CFK, regulation is putting money 'aside' for the athlete and his relatives. The regulation is fiscally founded on this basis (welfare idea). If the contract player dies, the CFK claims pass on to the lawful spouse or partner with whom the contract player lived. If the player does not have a partner, the funds are distributed to his child(ren). If the player is not married, does not have a partner, and does not have children registered with the CFK, no payments will be distributed according to the regulations and the money will benefit the other participants in the fund. If a player has been active as a contract player for one complete season, this player's family will – as long as he has not ended his career – receive a lifelong widow's pension on behalf of his wife and orphan's pension on behalf of his children, according to Article 10, Pension Scheme Rules and Regulations. Besides that, the player will – as soon as he ends his career – receive a temporary transitional pension and a lifelong retirement pension. Ending one's career involves only an actual ending and not a transfer to a foreign football club. A player may choose to continue adding to the fund during his stay in a foreign country. The foundation takes out collective insurance on behalf of the widows' and orphans' pension. The entitled parties are beneficiaries of this insurance; they receive a certificate of their claims. In case of the death of a contract player, his widow receives the still-remaining transitional pension.

§6. Dispute Settlement

I. Mediation

166. Mediation can be defined as a problem-solving method with help from a neutral third person, the mediator. This is an independent and impartial person whose task is to guide both parties to a solution which satisfies both parties. The formal arguments of the parties are not important in these negotiations; the parties' interests are the most important issues. The results of the negotiations will be placed in an agreement. There are two important conditions which must be fulfilled in order to have a successful mediation process. First, both parties need to be willing to solve the problem together. Second, the participants in the negotiations must be competent to reach an agreement. Mediation is based on two important starting points: voluntariness and confidentiality. No one can force participation in a mediation process.

II. Arbitration

167. Dutch law provides for the possibility of arbitration.[169] Arbitration has to be agreed on by the parties involved, for example, by means of a CLA or by means of articles of association;[170] it can be agreed upon while concluding the contract. Labour disputes can be resolved by means of arbitration, too. The arbitrator's judgment is binding upon all parties involved. Furthermore, it is possible to have a judgment (partially) quashed. This can only be achieved if the following limiting grounds apply:[171]

- there is no valid arbitration agreement;
- the arbitration tribunal was not constituted in a valid way;
- the arbitrators have exceeded their mandate;
- the judgment has not been signed in a legally valid manner or does it properly state the grounds on which it is based;
- the judgment or the way in which it has come about is contrary to public order or morality.

Furthermore, Dutch law provides for the possibility of a binding opinion from an appointed expert. This possibility has not been codified, so the parties can freely agree on the matter. However, once a binding opinion has been given, it is usually not easy to enforce. To this end, performance must be claimed before a civil court.

III. Courts

168. There are roughly three types of procedural law in the Netherlands. This includes the law of criminal procedure, the law of administrative procedure and the law of civil procedure. Every procedure applies to its own legal area. In labour law, the law of civil procedure and the law of administrative procedure are of particular importance. These will be discussed below. Furthermore, attention will be given to the possibilities of internal rules on the settlement of disputes, in the form of arbitration or a binding expert opinion. In conclusion, the arbitration rules of a number of sports associations, that have importance for the Netherlands, are examined.

A. Civil Proceedings

169. The employment contract is part of civil law. It is, after all, a 'common' contract. This means that the civil court has jurisdiction. The starting point for employment contracts is the subdistrict court of the district in which the labour is usually performed has jurisdiction. Moreover, the subdistrict court in the district in which the defendant has his residence is often competent as well. In principle, any

169. Article 1020 Rv.
170. *See*, for example, Art. 8, s. 3, articles of association KNVB.
171. Article 1065 Rv.

claim can be brought before a district court. For claims amounting up to EUR 25,000, and claims regarding consumer credit even up to EUR 40,000, rent disputes and labour disputes, the subdistrict courts are competent.

170. There are two types of proceedings, namely proceedings commenced by a writ of summons and proceedings commenced by an application. Proceedings commenced by a writ of summons involve a writ of summons, issued by a bailiff, that calls the defendant to appear in court at a certain date. On this date, the defendant may put up a written or verbal defence on the merits of the claim. The court can then pass judgment. Alternatively, this could mean the passing of a final judgment, an order to produce evidence, an order to appear in person or the provision of the possibility of the parties reciprocally reacting in writing. If necessary, the defendant in the proceedings may also enter a counterclaim.

171. Dutch law also provides for proceedings commenced by an application. These are relatively swift proceedings, implying the filing of a written application on which the opposing party subsequently submits a written reply. Generally, thereupon a hearing and the judgment follow. In labour law, this usually concerns the dissolution of an employment contract. In urgent cases, the court may be asked to issue a preliminary injunction.

172. Subsequently, commonly, one of the opposing parties may appeal from the judgment to the Court of Appeal. This judicial authority completely re-tries the case. After this, there is the possibility to bring the appeal to the Supreme Court of the Netherlands. This court solely examines whether a judgment of a lower court is contrary to the law or if there has been non-compliance with essential procedural requirements.

B. Legal Proceedings of Administrative Law

173. In case of government decisions, the conclusion and the subsequently applicable judicial process are governed by the General administrative law Act (Awb). This act indicates that besides the lawfulness of the decision, the government should also respect the general principles of proper administration, such as the prohibition of misuse of power, proper reasoning for the decision and due care. If someone disagrees with the decision of a government agency, this person should register a notice of objection to the decision with that government agency within six weeks after notification of the decision. The agency should then reconsider the decision internally. The decision after reconsideration should be given to the applicant in writing. The matter may then be submitted to the court of law within six weeks. After this, there is still a possibility of bringing the case to a higher (usually specialized) court. In urgent cases, the court may make provisional arrangements.

§7. MISCELLANEOUS

'Hooligan Law'

174. The legislation 'Measures to control football hooliganism and serious nuisance' (Wet MBVEO) is a Dutch act which came into force on 1 September 2010. The alternative names for this act are 'De Voetbalwet' or fully 'Amend the Municipalities Act, the Criminal Code and the Criminal Code regulating the powers of the mayor and the powers of the prosecutor to take measures to combat football hooliganism, serious nuisance or serious damaging behavior towards persons or property (measures to combat football hooliganism and serious antisocial behavior).' Although politicians have repeatedly called for tougher punishment, it took years to implement this law. The Dutch Football Association (de KNVB) has advocated for years for a special football law. On 30 June 2015 this legislation was tightened.

With this law both the mayor and the prosecutor have additional powers to intervene in hooliganism and serious antisocial behaviour. They can use this law to impose a lengthy exclusion order and/or a reporting requirement. An order lasts for three months and may be renewed up to three times per year. In addition, mayors have the possibility of prohibiting children from coming outside at night after 8 p.m. unless they are accompanied by a parent or guardian. The mayor can give parents the order to keep their children from entering a particular area.

Next to this, the prosecutor has extra powers. The prosecutor can impose people an exclusion order and a notification requirement to ensure that a person is in a particular part of the municipality. He can impose a restraining order which, for example, prevents that a victim unintentionally faces a perpetrator. The prosecutor can only do this if a person is suspected of a criminal offence. Finally, even those who assist in the preparation of committing violence against persons or property are punishable.

For example, with this law, supporter groups which agree to go to a certain spot to fight are punishable. Without the intervention of the court, the prosecutor can impose an exclusion order.

The effectuation of this law is the responsibility of municipalities, the public prosecution and the police.

The Municipalities Act already had an Article 172; the light command authority. The new Article 172a provides the mayor with the opportunity to give certain commands (so preventative) to a person who has repeatedly disrupted the public order individually or in groups or has had a leading role in severe fear of further disruption of the public order. Prohibited area can now be imposed prolonged.

I. Working Conditions

175. Partly due to the influence of the EU, the Netherlands provides for an extensive and detailed regulatory framework concerning working conditions. This concerns regulations provided by the government regarding labour circumstances. These regulations can particularly be found in the Working Conditions Act. This is a framework act, which means that the regulations of this act are worked out in greater detail by other regulations that are more specific. Hierarchically, the following image emerges:

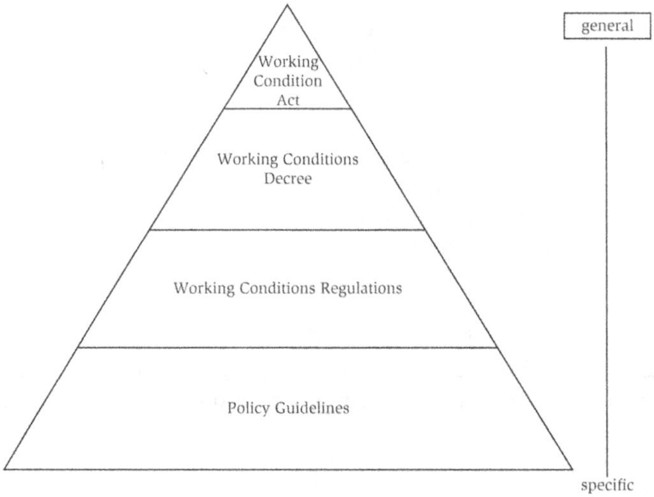

176. These regulations have a greater scope of application than just the employment contract. They apply to officials, activities conducted under authority, and working at home as well. Furthermore, these regulations not only impose obligations on the employer but also on the employee and the works council. Because of the complex nature of this legislation, we cannot discuss this act in detail. Only a rough outline will be set forth here.

177. The core of the act consists of the general duty of care of the employer for safe working conditions. This involves not only the safety of the workstation but the well-being of the employee in general as well. This last-mentioned duty of care concerns, among other things, the policy on sexual harassment, aggression, violence and alcohol abuse in the workplace. Moreover, the employer is under several specific obligations, among which are:

- risk overview and risk assessment;
- plan of action;
- information, schooling and supervision;
- appointing an employee in charge of preventing accidents;
- workplace help services.

178. In the Working Conditions Act the government has made a judicial framework for working conditions; employers and employees are given possibilities to create their own rules to fulfil the requirements of the act. This means that companies can make specific working condition rules so that the working conditions policy is customized to a specific area of labour. To make sure that the conditions set by the act are being followed, the labour inspector will react firmly to abuses of the act.

179. First of all, the employer should draft an overview of all the risks that are connected with labour. This should lead to a plan of action which describes measures that will be taken to remove these risks. Furthermore, a list of accidents in the workplace has to be maintained. In addition, severe accidents are to be reported to the Health and Safety Inspectorate; these are accidents which result in death, hospitalization or durable injury. Furthermore, the employer has the duty to register all the accidents that result in an employee's absence from work for more than three days. The employer is under the obligation to appoint aid workers within the company, too. These aid workers have the duty to render assistance in case of accidents, fire safety and evacuation. Furthermore, the employer is obliged to provide for a periodical medical examination insofar as this is of relevance to the performance of the particular type of labour. In accordance with the law, the employee is also under several obligations; for instance, the employee is obliged to respect safe working conditions.

A. The Ban on Smoking

180. As of 1 January 2014, there is a smoking ban in all buildings where employees are present during their duties. This ban ensues directly from the Tobacco Act (Article 10 section 1).

181. For the record, it is pointed out that the smoking ban does not apply to all employers.[172] The following exceptions to the ban on smoking exist:

- private spaces;
- open air.

The smoking ban is also applicable in restaurant, canteens, public buildings and public open spaces. As of July 2021 spaces for smoking are no longer allowed in public buildings. As of January 2022 this also applies for companies.

II. Working Hours

182. The Working Hours Act concerns the safety, health and well-being of the employee. This act and the Working Conditions Act make up a whole; these are framework acts. Hierarchically, the following arrangement applies:

Regulations provide for a standard regulatory framework which may be deviated from, usually only when the deviation is based on a CLA. Likewise, in some cases,

172. *See* Exception, Non-smoking Workplace Decree.

one may deviate from the standard regulatory framework by means of arrangements with the works council. The Labour Time Act covers the regulation of admissible labour times. The act allows for flexible labour times and agreements by company branch or venture. An important goal of the Labour Time Act is to widen the possibility to combine labour with tasks or activities outside the working climate. This does not mean that every employee has the right to change work hours according to personal wishes and circumstances. The act relating to part-time work (Wet flexibel werken) is more suitable in this respect; this act codifies under which conditions an individual employee can claim the right to shorten or extend hours of labour. During the determination of labour time and time for rest breaks, the Labour Time Act prescribes, however, a reasonable assessment of personal interests versus other company interests. The Labour Time Act establishes mandatory standards for the maximum number of hours that someone can work and for night labour. Deviation from this regulation by means of collective agreement is – excluding some exceptions – no longer possible. Only with regard to the number of hours of night duties is deviation possible to a limited extent.

183. Beside the Labour Time Act, the Labour Time Decision is in force. In this decision, specific regulations have been incorporated for special groups. The legislation, as codified in the Labour Time Act, is excluded in certain circumstances and in other situations, the legislation is extended. It is clear that in extreme circumstances such as natural disasters, serious accidents in shipping or aviation work settings, rules about maximum labour times are impossible to apply and, therefore, can be ignored. Special regulations apply to the aviation, shipping and transport industry. The legislation for these specific groups is not discussed in this monograph For additional information, please contact the relevant trade union or the Labour Inspectorate.

184. An employer is obligated, within the framework of the general venture policy, to make policy concerning labour and rest times. The employer must assess all interests within the enterprise against each other. The entrepreneur must establish risk identification and he has to evaluate the chosen regulation. The employer has to consult the works council on the policy. An employee who is of the opinion that within the pursued policy, his personal interests are suppressed in an unreasonable manner, can address the employer about this personally or through the representative advisory body or by its association. A legal procedure is possible.

185. In accordance with the Labour Time Act, the maximum labour time is twelve hours per period of labour and sixty hours a week. An employee can work an average of fifty-five hours a week, during a period of four weeks, and during a period of sixteen weeks an average of forty-eight hours a week.

186. The Labour Time Act stipulates that an employee must have a continuous rest time of at least eleven hours uninterrupted, per period of twenty-four hours. Only if the nature of the work or the company circumstances require otherwise, the time to rest can be shortened once during an uninterrupted period of 7 × 24 hours, to a minimum of eight hours.

187. The Labour Time Act gives employers and employees more freedom to make agreements regarding breaks. However, the act stipulates that:

- for a period of service of 5.5 hours, an employee is entitled to a break of at least thirty minutes (which can be split up into two breaks × fifteen minutes);
- for a period of work of ten hours, one is entitled to a break of at least forty-five minutes (which can be split up into three breaks × fifteen minutes).

188. 'On duty' means an unbroken period in which work is performed and which is located between two successive continuous times to rest of at least eight hours. In accordance with the Labour Time Act, the maximum labour time on duty is twelve hours a day and sixty hours a week. Only with respect to night duties has a maximum service duration been determined.

189. In the Labour Time Act, 'night duty' is a duty in which more than one hour of labour is performed between 12 p.m. and 6 a.m. If an employee starts before 5.45 a.m. it will no longer be referred to as night duty. The maximum duration of a night duty has been restricted to ten hours. The working week of the employee who frequently works at night is not allowed to work more than forty hours on average over a period of sixteen weeks and an employee may only work thirty-six night duties within sixteen weeks. It is possible to raise the number of night duties by agreement between employer and employee or by CLA up to 140 night duties a year.

190. 'Consignment' is a period between two shifts, in which the employee is not working but is required to be contactable. During emergencies or other unforeseen circumstances, he must be able to report to work as soon as possible. The Labour Time Act defines consignment as follows: 'consignment is a time space between two consecutive shifts or during a break, in which the employee is exclusively obliged to be contactable and in case of unforeseen circumstances he must perform work on recall as soon as possible'.

191. The strict regulations with respect to overtime in the Labour Time Act were removed as of 1 April 2007. Only one standard remains concerning the number of maximum hours that someone can perform labour.

192. The Labour Time Act does not address compensation for overtime. In practice, overtime compensation is an important matter. Provisions can be made by CLA or between the employer and employee. If these provisions have not been made, the circumstances under which overtime has been performed are decisive. Reasonableness, fairness and the obligation to act as a good employer are thereby important criteria. The Supreme Court has indicated that the overtime must be paid when the employer has been given the task to perform overtime; this task may be given tacitly. Therefore, an employee who himself decides to perform overtime does not satisfy this requirement. Many employers follow a rule that overtime will not be compensated for with money, but by means of 'time for time'.

193. The general rule in the Labour Time Act is that there will not be work on Sundays. Only if Sunday labour has been agreed to or when it is a result of the nature of the labour, it is permitted. No complete definition is given as to what must be understood under 'nature of labour'. Examples are: work at police force, fire brigade, catering industry, round-the-clock firms, farmer companies, public institutions, recreation sector and health care. It concerns, therefore, 'situations where it is logical and socially uncontested that there will be work on Sunday'.

In some cases, the company-bound circumstances can oblige labour on Sundays. Sometimes incidental Sunday labour is necessary, for example, when an order must be settled before a certain date. A circumstance in which the work takes place more structured, regular on Sunday, for instance, once a month, will lead to structured labour on Sundays. Sunday labour on the basis of the company circumstances mentioned above requires approval from the Works Council or other employee representation. After approval, there still will be consultation and collaboration required from every affected employee; the employee can refuse Sunday labour. A judge can eventually assess if the refusal is justified by weighing the reciprocal interests of the parties involved.

The position of the employee requested to work on Sundays due to company circumstances has considerably improved. In case the employee refuses, he does not need to give any reasons. It might concern religious practices, but also considerations having to do with the family or leisure activities. The only standard applied is that the refusal of the employee cannot be in conflict with the obligation of being a good employee. The necessary individual approval of the employee can only be requested once if it concerns structured Sunday labour because of company circumstances. In case of incidental labour on Sunday, the approval will be requested for each occasion.

194. In the Labour Time Act, children are defined as young people who have not reached the age of 16 years. The general rule is that children may not perform labour; their parents are also responsible for maintaining this labour prohibition. In a limited number of situations, the legislator has indicated that deviations from this labour prohibition are allowed in certain cases. Rules apply to different age categories.

195. Children of 13 and 14 years are allowed to work only for limited periods of time. For these children there is a difference between how much they are allowed to work during regular school weeks and during holiday weeks. During school weeks the principle is: the school takes precedence. It is the intention of the act to prevent 13- and 14-year olds regularly perform daily work besides attending school. For this reason, it has been decided that these children are allowed to perform a limited number of tasks incidentally. On school days, 13- and 14-year olds can perform 'jobs around the house and in the neighbourhood' for a maximum of two hours a day and a maximum of twelve hours a week. On a day off (Saturday and possible other day off) these children can do other types of work. This work consists of assistance services, and, therefore, cannot be independently performed work.

These rules have some exceptions. Children of tradesmen and farmers can work in the company of their parent(s) on school days for a maximum of two hours a day and twelve hours a week. This is only allowed because the workplace is the residence of the child. Children of 13 and 14 years can also participate in performances of a cultural, scientific, educational or artistic nature, in fashion shows or in audio-visual recordings. The rehearsals for the performances are also counted as work time.

196. Children of 14 years and older can perform work of a light nature within the framework of the educational setting. That is, however, only possible when there is a so-called training period agreement or when the mayor and aldermen have approved a request for replacing the learning time. A training period agreement must be signed by the parent/guardian of the child. If a child works within the framework of a training period or replacing learning time, he or she cannot perform other work during that week.

197. Children from the age of 15 years can perform non-industrial work of a light nature. They are allowed to work, outside study time and during the holidays for more hours than children of 13 and 14 years. Children of 15 years can also participate more often in performances. On Sunday, no work is performed unless:

- this is stipulated and Sunday work is a result of the nature of the labour;
- the company circumstances make working on Sunday necessary and the employer has agreed with the works council or other employee participation.

Note that the child can only work on Sundays if the parents or guardians explicitly give their authorization.

Children of 15 years or older who have been partially or entirely exempted from their learning time can do non-industrial work of a light nature. This does not concern working besides studying, but during (a part of) of the school year(s). In this situation special rules apply.

198. If all conditions are satisfied it is not necessary to put in a request for a licence at the Labour Inspectorate. One exception applies to this general rule, namely for children up to 13 years old. A licence must be acquired if they wish to take part in performances. It concerns particularly performances of cultural, scientific, educational or artistic nature or taking part in fashion shows and audio-visual recordings. The Labour Inspectorate, when granting a licence, must act in the best interests of the child.

199. 'Youthful employees' are employees who are 16 or 17 years old. Youthful employees are not allowed to perform night duties and cannot be faced with consignment. An important condition is that the labour and time-to-rest pattern of youthful employees must meet the requirement that he or she must be able to fulfil his or her learning duties. If a youthful employee works on Sunday, Saturday must be a day off. Within each period of seven twenty-four-hour periods, the youthful employee has to have a time to rest of at least thirty-six hours. Per period of twenty-four hours, the youthful employee must have a time to rest of at least twelve hours, between 11 p.m. and 6 a.m. Night duties have, therefore, been prohibited for youthful employees, just like overtime and consignment duties. If a youthful employee works for more than four and half hours, he is entitled to a break of at least a half-hour.

200. The Labour Time Act has some special rules for women, concerning work time as it relates to pregnancy and motherhood. The work of women who are pregnant or just gave birth must be changed so that their specific circumstances will be taken into account. A pregnant woman is entitled to extra breaks and is in principle not obligated to work night duties or overtime. A pregnant woman is also entitled to a regular and uniform work-and-rest pattern. From four weeks before the date of the childbirth up to ten weeks after the childbirth, the female employee does not have to perform any work. During the first nine months after birth the woman can interrupt her work to breastfeed or to express milk. The employer must make a suitable space available for this purpose in the workplace. The nursing mother is allowed a minimum of a quarter of her work time for this purpose, and the employer is obligated to pay for this time. If the nursing mother requires more time, the employer is not obligated to pay for this extra time.

III. Important Collective Agreement for Sports

A. The CLA for Trainer/Manager Professional Football

201.

(1) Its validity expires on 30 June 2022.
(2) It distinguishes the following functions:
   - technical director/ technical manager;
   - head of the youth academy;
   - head of scouting;
   - trainer/manager of the first team/assistant manager of the first team;
   - trainer/manager of the second team;
   - trainer/manager youth, sections A1, B1, C1;
   - specialized trainer.
(3) With regard to the specialized trainer and trainer/manager youth, other than sections A1, B1 and C1 this CLA can be used, but it is not mandatory. Deviation of the CLA is solely allowed in favour of the employee.
(4) A deviation is made from Article 7:668 A BW. It is permissible to conclude an unrestricted number of fixed-term employment contracts.
(5) Not later than 31 March of the year in which the employment contract comes to an end, it must be notified to the employee by registered letter whether the employment contract will be terminated. If not, the contract will repeatedly be extended for another year.
(6) Both parties are bound to a notice period of three months.
(7) Only an employment contract on a full-time basis may be concluded with an employee from outside the EU.

(8) The holiday allowance is 8%, with a maximum of three times the statutory minimum wages.
(9) During illness, the employee is allowed a maximum of fifty-two weeks at 100% wage. After those fifty-two weeks, the employee may receive a maximum of fifty-two weeks at 100% wage, unless the employee does not comply with the reintegration measures. If so the employee will only receive 70% of his wage. The obligation to continue payment lasts for a maximum of two years in total. In the premier division, a maximum of EUR 240,000 applies to calculate the continued payment of wages, while in the second division a maximum of EUR 90,000 applies.

B. The CLA for Professional Football Players in the Netherlands

202.

(1) Its validity expires on 30 June 2021.
(2) Employers: It applies to all BVOs, which means all the Dutch BVO that have a legal entity and have been admitted to compete in the Professional Football Competitions of the KNVB.
(3) Employees: It applies to all football players who have a labour contract (also known as player contract) with an employer mentioned above and has been registered as a contract player, has been registered with the section Professional Football of the KNVB to compete in the professional football leagues.
(4) Employment contracts are registered with the Royal Netherlands Football organization (Article 53 RBV).
(5) Employment contracts are always concluded for a definite period of time and always come to an end on 30 June of any year.
(6) The first employment contract rightfully ends after the defined period. From the time of the second employment contract, the employee must be given notice of termination. Under certain circumstances, a notice of termination by registered letter not later than 31 March is required.
(7) Employee must give a notice of termination by registered letter not later than 15 May.
(8) According to this CLA, a board of players can be established.
(9) Lending out a contract player is only allowed with approval of the employee himself.

Part III. Sport Disputes and Disciplinary Procedures

203. Sports cannot exist without a set of rules which are abided by all the participants. Supervision on compliance with these rules differs from sport to sport and is often in the hand of referees or jurors. Violations can occur and be punished during a game but can also be – depending on the nature of the violation – be punishable afterwards, i.e., by means of imposing suspension of several matches or a deduction of points. It is also possible misbehaviour occurs of the field by spectators, clubs or managers.

§1. Disciplinary Law in Sports

204. Sanctioning of misbehaviour and violation of the rules is possible through disciplinary law, which is, in contrast to disciplinary law, which is legislated like for instance for doctors or lawyers, in general not regulated by any special laws. Disciplinary law in sports is left to the (international) sports organizations and is therefore (in principle) not regulated by law but exists within the boundaries of rules governing associations (*see* paragraph 9). Everyone who becomes a member of a sports club automatically accepts to be subjected to the rules within that club or organization and its own internal legal order.

205. Often sports clubs have mandated the authority to impose disciplinary action to internal and independent bodies or committees.[173] The competence and ways of working are laid down in the by-laws of these clubs. In the Netherlands most disciplinary systems exist of two layers: a disciplinary committee in first instance and a committee of appeal in second instance. Furthermore, in some cases, the Court of Arbitration for Sport (CAS) in Lausanne, Switzerland, is open to appeal procedures. In recent years some sports federations have instated public defenders who can offer plea bargains to relieve the disciplinary system. This is the case at the KNVB a recently at the Royal Dutch Swimming Association (KNZB).

A verdict in disciplinary law can be qualified as a (civil) decision of a body of the association (Article 2:9 DCC) or a binding advise by means of Article 7:900 section 2 CC. Sometimes disciplinary law is part of an arbitration procedure and therefore

173. S.F.H. Jellinghaus (red.), *Capita Sportrecht,* Antwerpen/'s-Hertogenbosch: Gompel & Scavina 2021, p. 87.

subjected to the rules on arbitration (Article 1094 Act on Legal Actions). Scholars have not yet reached a common opinion on this matter; the authors however lean towards qualification as a decision of a body of the association.[174]

If a member disagrees with the verdict and no internal appeal is possible, he can go to public court to have the verdict annihilated. This is only possible on rare occasions and almost never happens. This is possible when the decision is in conflict with by-laws or statutes of the club, or is not reasonable or fair (Article 2:15 CC). The court will review whether the disciplinary body could have reasonably come to this decision. The decision is thus reviewed only marginally. First question is whether the internal procedures have been followed correctly; second whether general principles of law have been followed in the procedure. Article 6 of the European Treaty on Human Rights is not directly applicable, since this is a civil and strictly internal procedure, but the basic principles following from this article must be taken into account. Such as; the presumption of innocence, the right to a fair trial, equality of arms and due process. The right to a public hearing is usually not a right that is applicable in disciplinary law.[175]

In the Netherlands some smaller sports associations (like the Badminton, Fencing and Surfing Association) are connected to the Institute for Sport Adjudication (ISR). This is an organization to which these associations can outsource their disciplinary procedures. It also deals with match fixing, sexual harassment and doping. The ISR also reviews whether or not an athlete is eligible for a subsidy for legal representation during disciplinary procedures.

To illustrate the magnitude of disciplinary law in the Netherlands; in 2018 the KNZB handled in total 1.122 cases of physical and oral misconduct during and surrounding sports matches, of which 766 led to a penalty.[176] Recent numbers are available at the website of the KNZB, but do not provide a representative image due to the cancellation of the competition due to the corona virus.

§2. Dispute Settlement in Sports

206. Next to internal disciplinary procedures, most sports associations have administrative procedures for settling disputes between or with their members. For instance, the KNVB has an in-house Arbitration Committee. This committee is solely competent (thus with exclusion of the civil courts) to judge on all disputes related to football, between or with members of the KNVB or intermediaries.

For example a dispute was settled in 2019 between an athlete and an intermediary about the explanation of the contract for representation. The Committee judged that the athlete was free to negotiate his own transfer and was not obliged to pay

174. *See* on this matter, D. Schwartz & G.A. Hahn, '*Een introductie tot het tuchtrechtelijke proces in het waterpolo*', TvSR 2020, 1/2.
175. *See* on this matter, D. Schwartz & G.A. Hahn, '*Een introductie tot het tuchtrechtelijke proces in het waterpolo*', TvSR 2020, 1/2.
176. Jaarverslag KNZB 2018.

damages to the intermediary for not using her services in opposition to the contract.[177] Because this procedure is an arbitration procedure, the rules on arbitration procedures of the Code of Civil Legal actions are applicable. Because both athletes and intermediaries are bound by the by-laws of the KNVB (and FIFA), they are obliged to agree with the competency of the committee. This means parties are not allowed to pass the Committee and go to civil court (Article 1022 Code on Civil Legal Actions). Judgment of the Committee is binding and no appeal is possible at CAS. If the parties in dispute do not agree with the judgment of the Committee, they can start a civil procedure to nullify the verdict. This is only possible on the ground of Article 1065 Code on Civil Legal Actions when:

- there are no legal grounds to settle the dispute by arbitration;
- the Committee is not composed in compliance with the rules;
- the Committee exceeded its competency;
- the verdict is not signed or motivated;
- the verdict is in conflict with general rules of 'public order'.

As a result of the above-mentioned grounds, an annihilation of the verdict is only possible on formal grounds and the procedure in civil court is therefore not an appeal. In principle such a procedure has to be started within three months after the verdict has been sent to the parties (Article 1064a Code on Civil Legal Actions).

Not all sports associations have their internal dispute settlement based on arbitration. For example the KNZB has the same committee for disciplinary procedures preside over internal disputes. An example of such a dispute is a case in 2020 where the manager of the competition punished a team for playing waterpolo with a player who was not allowed to play (because she played in another foreign competition). The punishment was a deduction of three points. The club disagreed with this decision and 'sued' the manager of the competition to reverse the deduction. The committee judged that this complaint was brought too late and therefore not admissible.[178] This decision was later appealed and the Committee of Appeal did find the complaint to be admissible.[179] Because this is not an arbitration procedure, the rules of the Code on Civil Legal Actions does not apply. Instead the legal framework set out in the previous paragraph is applicable.

The above-mentioned ISR does also offer dispute settlement. This can be in the form of arbitration, mediation or a binding advise.

§3. Doping and Sports

207. In 2018 the Law on Execution of the Anti-doping Policy (WUAB) came into force and it regulates the Doping Authority which is established on 1 January 2019. The goal of the Doping Authority is to realize sports in the Netherlands without any doping. The Doping Authority is charged with:

177. KNVB College van Arbiters 12 Jul. 2019, nr. 1500.
178. KNZB Tuchtcommissie 29 Jan. 2020, TU2020-001.
179. Commissie van Beroep, 10 Mar. 2020, BER 20-009.

- Fighting the use of doping in sports.
- Carrying out doping checks-procedure (i.e., making decisions on the composition of the top sport group, taking part in disciplinary procedures, and taking body samples).
- Collecting and researching information about possible violations of the doping regulations.
- Educating about doping.

On the basis of the WUAB athletes are obliged to cooperate with the test. The Doping Authority works on the basis of the World Anti-Doping Code and only focuses on doping by humans only. Animals like horses and doves are not within the jurisdiction of the authority. Furthermore, the actual carrying out of the tasks of the authority is done on the basis of the National Doping regulation. All sports associations have to include this regulation in their by-laws.

208. In addition, there are general laws, particularly the Opium Act, the Medicines Act and several provisions of the Penal Code and the Economic Offences Act. In addition, one should look at the regulations of the (international) sporting associations. The regulations are in effect in pursuance of the membership relationship.[180] With regard to the working relationship, a specific situation must also be looked at on the basis of 'common' labour law to determine in what way one should deal with a specific doping situation. There is as yet no definitive case law on this subject.

209. In the author's opinion, the employer is not allowed to compel the sportsman/ employee based on the right of instruction to use drugs or illegal narcotics. This ensues primarily from the legislation on working conditions and the principle of good employership. Furthermore, the employment contract usually contains the provision that the sportsman/employee is a member of the sporting association, of which the employer is usually a member as well. In accordance with this, the sportsman/employee cannot be compelled to act in violation of the anti-doping provisions of the association.

210. If the employer finds out that his employee has been involved in doping without his permission, there is, in the author's opinion, in principle sufficient reason to (instantly, if necessary) dismiss the employee. This results from the fact that in such a case the employee has acted contrary to the contents of the employment contract (in which are incorporated anti-doping provisions).[181] All this, even apart from the possibility of penalties imposed by the association, including suspension.

211. In late 2003, the General Assembly of the Dutch sporting umbrella organization NOC*NSF adopted the World Anti-Doping Code. As a result, Dutch sporting associations were obliged to bring their regulations into conformity with this

180. *See*, for example, Arbitration Tribunal KNVB, 30 Oct. 1997, Sportzaken 1997/4 No. B10.
181. Cf. Sub-district Court Rotterdam, 22 Feb. 1993, JAR 1993, 103.

Code before August 2004. Dutch Center for Doping issues (NECEDO) has, in cooperation with all parties concerned, drawn up model doping regulations based on the model doping code created by the World Anti-Doping Agency (WADA). NECEDO merged in 2006 with the Dutch Doping Control (DOCONED) to form the Foundation Anti-Doping Authority in the Netherlands, which in turn changed into the Doping Authority. At present the National Doping regulation is the leading document for the Doping Authority. A violation of the National Doping regulation is, practically speaking, the use of one or more substances or methods named on the WADA doping list. A substance or method will be placed on the doping list if it satisfies two of the following three criteria:

(1) It is intended to intensify performance.
(2) It is harmful to the sportsman's health.
(3) It is against 'the spirit of sport', meaning in contradiction to the standards and values of sport, such as fair play.

A new anti-doping code (NDR 2021) came into force as of 1 January 2021. In short, some important changes are the fact that disciplinary action taken against the use of doping may only be organized outside of the own federation. In the Netherlands this means only ISR is competent to review anti-doping cases. Next to the discouraging of sporters or others to report misuse of doping has been made punishable. Also new ways of punishing have come into force.

When a sportsman is a first offender, he can be sentenced with a disqualification of up to four years. During this period, the sportsman is not allowed to participate in any game or training schedule. And when the use of doping occurs in a game, the sportsman will be disqualified from the game results and must hand in his medals, prize money points, etc.

A second violation of the doping code can lead to an increase of the first sanction, whereby the disqualification is at least six months up to twice the time of the first disqualification, while a third violation of the doping code usually will lead to a lifetime disqualification.

When a number of sportsmen of a team violate the doping code, the whole team can be disqualified or otherwise sanctioned. In 2019, 2,427 drug tests were administered in the Netherlands. In 1.2% of the cases an abnormality had been found.[182] The following graph illustrates the development of abnormalities found after a doping test:

182. Jaarraportage 2019 Dopingautoriteit.

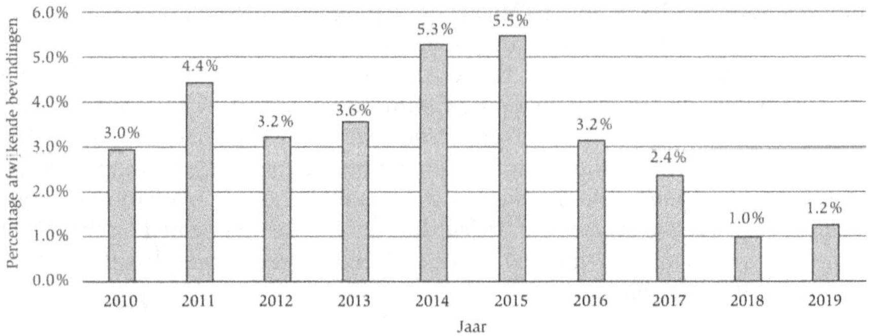

A sportsman is considered guilty of doping from the moment his urine sample is tested positive. In such a case, the sportsmen will be judged by the committee that organized the sporting event. After that judgment, the sportsman can appeal to the CAS.

Part IV. Sports and Commerce

Chapter 1. The Commercial Portrait Right of the Athlete

§1. Introduction: Commercial Interest

212. Publication (of a portrait) is not allowed, in so far as the person portrayed has a reasonable interest in opposing its publication, according to Article 21 of the Dutch Copyright Act (AW or Auteurswet), which forms the basis of the Dutch portrait right. A portrait is an image on which the person portrayed is recognizable. Initially, the portrait right merely intended to protect the privacy of the person portrayed: only the interest of privacy was considered a 'reasonable interest' in the sense of Article 21 AW.

In 1979, in the *Schaep met de Vijf Pooten*[183] judgment, the HR broadened its scope by adding the commercial interest:

> Although when drawing up the Copyright Act the legislator must mainly have had in mind interests of a non-financial nature when using the words 'a reasonable interest' in article 21, a reasonable interest may also exist – in view of the relevant development of opinions in society – if the popularity of person portrayed, acquired in the exercise of his profession, is such that the commercial exploitation of that popularity is made possible by any form of publication of their portraits. The interest of those portrayed, to receive the benefits of said exploitation, without having to consent to the publication of their portraits for commercial purposes without receiving a fee for said publication is a reasonable interest in the sense of art. 21.

213. From that moment on, and in addition to a privacy portrait right, a commercial portrait right has existed in the Netherlands for individuals who had a 'cashable popularity'.[184] Prior to that[185] and after that,[186] many well-known athletes successfully invoked their commercial portrait rights.

---

183. HR 19 Jan. 1979, NJ 1979, 383 m.nt. LWH, AMR 1979, 52 m.nt. JHS (met ill.), BIE 1979, nr 23, 163 ('t Schaep met de Vijf Pooten).
184. Hof 's-Gravenhage 13 Apr. 1960, NJ 1961, 160.
185. Pres. Rb. 's-Gravenhage 17 Feb. 1965, BIE 1966, nr 14, 44 (Voetballer Donners); Pres. Rb. 's-Gravenhage 7 Dec. 1965, BIE 1966, nr 66, 240 (Feyenoordspelers); Pres. Rb. Haarlem 26 Jun. 1974 (twee zaken), NJ 1974, 415, BIE 1977, nr 3, 11 en nr 4, 13 (De slag om het voetbalgoud).

§2. Use in Advertising

214. In 1997, in its *Discodanser* judgment, the Supreme Court considered:[187]

> that the protection of art. 21 AW provided to those portrayed, especially against infringements of their right of privacy, implies that the person portrayed will basically always have a reasonable interest in opposing the use of his portrait in commercial advertising.

215. This leads to the conclusion that unknown citizens, including the unknown (amateur) athlete, may oppose the use of his portrait in advertising because this use may lead to the false impression that he would endorse the product. The privacy portrait right is indirectly used to give anonymous citizens a kind of commercial portrait right, which may be considered an expansion of the portrait right.

216. In 2020 the court of Amsterdam judged that a professional football player was supposed to have given his consent to use his image to promote collectible 'football images' as advertisement by a large supermarket. This consent was derived from the CLA which was applicable on the labour agreement with the football player.[188]

§3. Notion of 'Portrait'

217. In 2003, in the *Breekijzer*[189] judgment, the Supreme Court expanded the notion of portrait by ruling as follows:

> Making (part of) the face of the person portrayed unrecognisable does not necessarily mean that this does not constitute a portrait in the sense of 21 AW, since the identity of that person may become clear from the rest of the illustration, and therefore publication of such an illustration may be prohibited on the basis of this provision.

218. This clearly stretches the notion of 'portrait' in comparison with the *Ja zuster, nee zuster*[190] and *Naturiste*[191] judgments, in which it was still a requirement that (part of) the face be shown.

---

186. I.e.: Pres. Rb. Utrecht 16 Jan. 1980, NJ 1980, 481 (Krol c.s./Panini); Ktr. Harderwijk 29 May 1991, AMI 1991, 206, Mf 1991, B115, Prg. 3507 (Kramer/Burnham) HR 14 Jun. 2013, NJ 2015/112 m. nt. P.B. Hugenholtz, Rechtbank Amsterdam 15 Apr. 2015, ECLI:NL:RBAMS:2015:2103.
187. HR 2 Mayi 1997, NJ 1997, 661 m.nt. DWFV, AMI 1997, 143 m.nt. Schuijt, Mf 1997, B104.
188. Rechtbank Noord-Holland 29 Occt. 2020, ECLI:NL:RBNO:2020:8553.
189. HR 12 May 2003, NJ 2004, 80 m.nt. EJD, AMI 2003, nr 14, 175 m.nt. Hugenholtz, Mf 2003, nr 30, 211 m.nt.
190. HR 16 Jan. 1970, NJ 1970, 220 m.nt. GJS; AA 1970, 377 (met ill.) m.nt. Cohen Jehoram, BIE 1971, nr 24, 122 m.nt. SB.
191. NJ 1988, 277 m.nt. LWH, AMI 1988, 58 m.nt. Bunschoten. Zie de afbeelding in AMI 1986, 60.

219. For example, The *Ja zuster, nee zuster* judgment, in which a recognizable face was a defining requirement for a portrait, was superseded by the *Breekijzer* judgment.

For example, the same applies to the *Naturiste* judgment, in which a 'characteristic body posture' was a requirement.

This stretching of the concept of a 'portrait' is illustrated clearly in the case of Riot Games/Edgar Davids. In the computer game 'League of Legends' an avatar was available which had the distinct looks of the Dutch football player Edgar Davids. This avatar was called 'Striker Lucian'. The court judged that the underlying technique is of no significant meaning for the question of whether or not something is a portrait:

> It is the combination of all elements; dark skin, sporty figure, aggressive style of playing, black dreadlocks and sporting glasses combined with a football uniform which makes the skin of Striker Lucian a portrait of Edgar Davids. The public will – in the more detailed pictures of Striker Lucian – recognize the image of Edgar Davids.[192]

§4. Consequences of Broader Scope

220. The expansions of the portrait right in the *Discodanser* and *Breekijzer* cases have had their effects in practice and lower jurisdiction.

I. *J-Peetje*

221. Worth mentioning is the *J-Peetje* judgment of the District Court of Amsterdam.[193] Politicians do not usually invoke their portrait rights and accept commercial use of their portraits. Former Prime Minister Balkenende, however, considered it necessary to take action (in the name of the State) against an advertisement of Kijkshop, in which he was depicted as a young child, with the accompanying text: 'Without a shop assistant J-Peetje shops cheaper'.

222. Nobody thought that the Prime Minister had consented to this ad, or that he would endorse the product (a Senseo coffee machine). However, the Court of Amsterdam ruled that the mere association between a product and a person portrayed, including the Prime Minister, may be prohibited.

At first sight it seems as if the Court of Amsterdam simply applied the new *Discodanser* ruling quoted above. But the Supreme Court added the following to the ruling quoted above:

192. Rb. Amsterdam 9 Aug. 2017, ECLI:NL:RBAMS:2017:5415.
193. Rb. Amsterdam 2 Feb. 2005, Mediaforum 2005/3, 125, IER 2005, 44 (Staat/Kijkshop; Balkenende).

> Including a portrait in an ad for a product or service therefore will result in the public making an association between the person portrayed and that product or service, in which case the public will generally, and usually correctly assume that the portrait has not been used without the approval of the person portrayed, and will interpret the use of the portrait in the ad as a sign of public endorsement of the product or service by the person portrayed. For these reasons using a portrait in such a way is basically an infringement of the privacy of the person portrayed. That means that a reasonable interest as referred to in art. 21 AW exists, which opposes such publication.

This reasoning, however, is not found in the judgment of the Court of Amsterdam:

> The protection given by article 21 to the person portrayed, in this case Balkenende, in particular against infringement of his privacy, implies that the person portrayed will basically always have a reasonable interest in opposing his portrait being used without his permission in advertising. The objection to being associated with commercial activities of a different person is in itself basically a violation of privacy, and results in a reasonable interest as referred to in article 21 AW.

A. *Suggestion of Public Endorsement Required or Not?*

223. It is clear that the Court of Amsterdam in the above-mentioned case left out an important and possibly essential step in the considerations of the Supreme Court: the fact that the public will interpret the case as a 'public endorsement':

> Matters are not different for politicians who, for reasons of their position, cannot commercially use their portrait, such as Balkenende. Because of his position in our former government he may have reasonable objections against the use of his portrait for commercial purposes by an individual enterprise, without being asked for permission. It is not a requirement that the recipients of brochures and the shopping public assume that Balkenende has personally cooperated in or has received money for the advertising campaign.

With this last consideration, the Court suggests that it is not relevant whether the public will assume that the portrait will not be used without the *approval* of Balkenende, and will interpret the use of the portrait in the advertising message as a *sign of public endorsement* of the product or service by Balkenende. But that is not certain, because 'cooperation' differs from 'approval' and 'receiving money' differs from 'showing public endorsement'.

B. Is Association Sufficient?

224. But in this advertisement this does not make much difference: nobody will ever assume that Balkenende had given his approval or that he would wish to publicly endorse Kijkshop in this manner. That is an essential difference with the *Discodanser* case. The court, however, disregarded that: anybody always has the right to oppose the use of his portrait in advertising; any suggested approval or endorsement is not relevant. It is sufficient that 'an association, whether implied or not, is created'.

This expansion of the scope of *Discodanser* seems unfortunate to the author. It is quite plausible that even more people will bring claims if their portraits are used in advertising. In the author's opinion, there are supporting arguments for, in case of derogatory and prominent use of anonymous citizens, and athletes and artists may invoke their commercial portrait right. In the author's opinion, politicians should certainly have to accept the publicity, as long as this does not lead to deceiving or confusing the public. 'Creating an association, whether implied or not' is in the author's opinion too weak a ground to grant a politician the right to prohibit the use of his portrait. Politicians are simply part of the public domain.

The absolute application of the privacy portrait right in case of advertising as represented by the Court of Amsterdam could result in claims in connection with all kinds of coincidental, innocent use of portraits (groups of people in the image, passers-by in commercials). Claims such as these, which are frequent already, are not usually submitted to the judge, but are settled for several hundreds or thousands euros. In this way, the privacy portrait right will in practice be exercised as a commercial portrait right. Combined with the portrait right expanded by the *Breekijzer* ruling (namely, anything which may result in recognition is a portrait), the number of claims in connection with portrait rights of anonymous citizens could increase even more.

II. Katja Schuurman: Look-Alike and Parody Defence

225. The notion of a portrait, which was drastically expanded by the HR in a privacy portrait right case, was first applied in a commercial portrait right case in the case of Katja Schuurman (a Dutch television celebrity) and the 'GoudenGids' (a Dutch phonebook). In the past, it was disputed whether portrait right also applied to look-alikes,[194] although this was often solved by the use of the action against a wrongful act and the notion of the portrait with a 'minor difference'.[195] Also interesting is the parody defence, which has had its own place in the AW since 2004.

226. Although in the case of Katja there may have been characteristic hair and the 'characteristic body posture' of the *Naturiste* judgment, the court stresses that

194. Zie: Pres. Rb. Amsterdam 22 Dec. 1994, AMI 1995, 136 (met ill.) m.nt. JHS, Mf 1995, B19 (met ill.), IER 1995, nr 12, 61 (met ill.) (Millecam-look-alike).

195. Pres. Rb. Amsterdam 4 Feb. 1977, NJ 1977, 280 (Sonja Barend) en Hof Amsterdam 2 Nov. 1977, NJ 1978, 333 (Willeke Alberti).

since *Breekijzer* 'a portrait is also deemed to exist if there are no resembling facial features but other identifying factors'. The look-alike defence was rejected, as was the case of deliberate resemblance that is in accordance with the new, wider scope of the notion of 'portrait'. With this, the commercial portrait right seems to become almost as broad as the protection of well-known brands: an association with the person portrayed seems to be sufficient.

The judge rejected the parody defence because (a) no humour was involved, 'since (b) reasons of commercial competition have been crucial and (c) there is a clear danger of confusion':

(a) No humour? With this the judge steps on thin ice (in the author's opinion unnecessarily in this case). What is humour? The ad is amusing, or was in any event intended to be humorous ('turning one's back', a suit of banknotes instead of pages from the Gouden Gids). In the author's opinion, a judge should not jump to the conclusion of whether something is humorous or not. He should preferably limit himself to verifying whether the objective was to be humorous, and should not apply this too strictly.
(b) Commercial reasons? It is obvious that in this case there were commercial objectives, and this should be taken into account in the judgment. An independent comedian, columnist or caricaturist should have a greater margin of freedom than a competitor. In spite of this, the author feels that the commercial reasons, in this case comparative advertising, should not in all cases prevent acceptable parody. In case of an (alleged) parody which is sold on a large scale for a long time as an independent product (cf. Harry Potter/Tanja Grotter[196]), 'commercial reasons' will presumably often rule out acceptable parody. In the case of a temporary advertising campaign, a parody should be accepted much more easily.
(c) Risk of confusion? This is certainly relevant in judging a parody. If the public may actually be confused, and may think that it is the real thing, parody cannot be accepted. It is doubtful, however, whether that was the case in the mentioned verdict. Even if at first sight a moment of confusion would be created, the parody should not be immediately prohibited for that reason. The nice thing about parody is that we may think for a moment that it is real.

227. Should the advertisement with the conscious parody have been allowed? Because (in the author's opinion) it was indeed humorous, and because there is no risk of actual confusion, and the commercial reasons are not prohibitive in this case, and given the temporary character (including the promise not to repeat this), the author would answer this question affirmatively for reasons referred to in the valedictory speech of Verkade, '*Het belang van een bagatel*'.

Nevertheless, the advertisement was rightly prohibited because it appears that it was misleading advertising. Comparative advertising is allowed, but making incorrect and misleading claims in advertising is not allowed; not in the form of parody, either. Incidentally, the defendant may have been the big winner, in fact, thanks to

196. Hof Amsterdam 6 Nov. 2003, AMI 2004, nr 4, 36 m.nt. Klomp, IER 2004, nr 20, 119 m.nt. MdCB, LJN AN7646 (Harry Potter/Tanja Grotter).

a lot of free publicity, whereas the plaintiff, Gouden Gids, will have a severe hangover since its colour trademarks were declared practically invalid.

The parody defence is also raised in cases concerning sportsmen. In 2017 supermarket Jumbo sued the grocery delivery company Picnic for using in their commercials a look-a-like of the Dutch Formule-1 driver Max Verstappen, who appeared in tv-commercials of Jumbo. The court (court of appeals) judged that the commercial with Max Verstappen was 'clearly a parody that was intended to be humorous'.[197] When the case was tried in the underlying procedure, the court judged that this look-a-like in fact was a portrait of Max Verstappen: '*A portrait is not per definition a specific person, but an aid which helps bring up the image of this specific person. (…) In this case Picnic used a look-a-like with all the characteristic features of the portrait of [plaintiff 2]: same cap, same racing outfit, same hair color, same silhouette and same posture.*'[198] This verdict held up in appeal in 2020.[199]

§5. Other Developments

I. Portrait Right and Match Images

228. Early in 2004, the District Court of Amsterdam gave a judgment in a case that did not have to do with the expansion of the portrait right as initiated by the Supreme Court, but which, had the judgment been different, could have resulted in a different expansion of the portrait right.[200]

229. Can professional football players claim a fee for televised matches on the basis of Article 21 AW? Have players expressly or implicitly given their approval for the broadcasting? The Court of Amsterdam considered:

> Just as the clubs and the KNVB (Dutch Football Association) the Court considers that this approval is basically included in the employment agreements entered into by and between the professional football players and their clubs. It is part of the agreed, paid performance of labour of a professional football player that he takes part in matches that may be used for profit for the benefit of his employer. Said use has taken place by broadcast of matches for dozens of years. The players must be deemed to have taken that into account when signing their employment agreements.

That could only have been different if portrait rights for this type of situation would have been expressly acknowledged by clubs and/or KNVB, but according to the Court this does not appear from minutes and decisions of the KNVB, and not by the 'image contracts' of the clubs, either.

---

197. Vzr. Rechtbank Amsterdam 13 Okct. 2016, ECLI:NL:RBAMS:2016:9747, Hof Amsterdam 2 May 2017, ECLI:NL:GHAMS:2017:1722.
198. Rb Amsterdam 6 Sep. 2017, ECLI:NL:RBAMS:2017:6395.
199. Gerechtshof Amsterdam, 2 Jun. 2020, ECLI:NL:GHAMS:2020:1410.
200. Rb. Amsterdam 25 Feb. 2004, Spelers/Clubs en KNVB, AMI 2004, 107.

II. Commercial Portrait Right and Charity

230. Although inconsistent at first sight, the commercial portrait right also applies to its use of non-commercial purposes, such as charity. That was the conclusion of the Court of Amsterdam in the case involving the book *Jongensdromen* (*Boys' Dreams*):[201]

> The popularity of players gives them the opportunity to cash in on that popularity. That requires them to safeguard the exclusiveness of their portraits. That exclusiveness is also a matter of consideration if their portraits are used for charity. This interest of the players in the protection of the exclusiveness of their portraits and their value is based on article 21 of the 'Auteurswet 1912' and the approval referred to in said article. The players can and may manage the publication of their portraits in such a way that they will keep their value for a specific purpose. That also applies to portraits being used for charity. If this were different, unrestricted use by charities would result in loss of the exclusive value, also for those charities. So basically, it is the option of the players to determine whether and for which purpose their portraits are used in order to safeguard that value.

231. The dispute concerned *Jongensdromen*, a book containing images of the portraits of most players on the Dutch national soccer team. The players were photographed in a sleeping position, from late 2003 to early 2004. Each photo was accompanied by text written by a well-known journalist, columnist or author. The proceeds of the book were to go to the Foundation 'Spieren voor Spieren' (Muscles for Muscles), which tries to find funds for scientific research into muscular disorders. The facts showed that cooperation was given to taking these photos, but that no permission was given for their publication in the form of the above book. That again confirmed that permission to make portraits does not imply approval of (any form of) publication.

III. 'Greatest Goals'

232. At the end of 2007, in an action brought by Marco van Basten (a Dutch soccer player), the Court of Amsterdam prohibited a DVD containing 'Greatest Goals of all Times', produced by Dutch Filmworks.[202] It was remarkable that the judge not only prohibited the use of a photo of Marco van Basten on the DVD cover, but the entire DVD itself, containing footage of twenty-nine goals scored by van Basten, and more than 200 goals scored by other players. The judge considered:

> A reasonable financial interest does not only depend on the fact that the use can be characterized as merchandising or advertising, but whether it is a form

201. Vzr. Rb. Amsterdam 12 May 2004, KNVB en Oranje-spelers/ Being There ('Jongensdromen') AMI 2004, 107, LJN-nr. AO9324.
202. Vzr. Rb. Amsterdam 5 Dec. 2007, Van Basten/Filmworks, AMI 2008, 41 m.nt. Pinckaers.

of use that exclusively or mainly intends commercially use a person's cashable popularity. That may not be the case – always depending on the context – if the portrait is used as an illustration in a publication intended to provide information about the (history of) football, a football tournament or a certain club. The DVD of Dutch Filmworks however, has a different character. It is a compilation of goals which are not intended as an illustration to a subject, but are the essence of the product. Apart from the performances shown – not the subject of the dispute – each time a portrait of the scoring player is used, in any case as far as the goals of Van Basten's are concerned. Without the use of the portraits the product would not exist, and the goals are each time expressly linked to the scoring player. Further, Van Basten's goals are among the highlights of the DVD, which is stressed by his portrait on the cover of the DVD. In this way Van Basten's popularity is cashed, and he may oppose that on the basis of a reasonable financial interest. Unlike Dutch Filmworks feels, this does not lead to the situation that Van Basten owns the exclusive rights in the footage of his goals and/or would have the right to restrict the freedom of information. This action merely addresses the method of use by Dutch Filmworks; other methods of use require a separate judgment, which may lead to different conclusions.

233. The conclusion reached is that in certain circumstances a compilation of sports footage, if it is expressly linked to a single athlete who has achieved commercial popularity, may be prohibited on the basis of the commercial portrait right.

§6. Summary and Conclusion

234. In past decades, the portrait right of both well known and unknown athletes has been considerably expanded. First, the notion of 'portrait' was given a much broader scope: an action invoking portrait right does not require that part of a face and/or a characteristic posture are shown. A characteristic setting or other features in an illustration may turn an illustration into a portrait. Deliberate look-alikes are definitely subject to portrait rights. For unknown athletes, it is relevant that they too may prohibit the use of their portrait in advertising. Incidentally, it is not yet clear whether, and if, well known or unknown athletes would have to accept use in the setting of a parody. In case of commercial use (for advertising), this will probably not easily be the case. The scope of the portrait right is not yet such that players, whose essential performance consists of playing in front of television cameras, may demand an additional fee for the fact that their portrait is broadcast. Well known (and possibly also lesser-known) athletes, however, may oppose the use of their portraits for non-commercial/charity purposes without their permission. In certain circumstances, well-known athletes can oppose the use of compilations of sports footage, such as goals, if these are expressly linked to their commercial popularity.

COVID-19 and Its Impact on National Sport[203]

235. The COVID-19 pandemic has far-reaching consequences for our society. Also the Dutch sports sector is facing problems due to the health crisis; different measures to counteract the corona infections make practising a sport more difficult and complicated. Sports associations and clubs have financial problems and top-level sports have been at a standstill for a while. This contribution provides an overview of the current most important measures, regulations and financial support that affect the Dutch sports sector.

Regulations and Measures

236. The Dutch government has taken several measures for the sports sector to prevent corona infections during sports. The measures have changed throughout the pandemic, taking into account the threat and situation at the time. In principle everyone was only allowed to play sports outside. The dressing rooms, showers and canteens of sports clubs were closed, indoor sports facilities remained closed and no one was allowed to be present at training sessions and matches. Therapeutic sports were allowed, such as rehabilitation. Currently no measures are in force anymore.

The measures varied by sport and age. The government is trying to give young adults more space to be socially and physically active, partly in view of their mental and physical well-being. Children and youth up to 17 years had the most freedom in the field of sports. They were allowed to play sports together outdoors anywhere and did not have to keep 1.5 m distance. They were also allowed to play matches with teams from their own sports association. However, matches between clubs were not allowed. Young adults from 18 to 26 years old were allowed play sports outdoors with a maximum of two people at a distance of 1.5 m. At sports facilities and other locations (on the initiative of the municipality), they could practice outdoor sports together. They did not have to keep a distance of 1.5 m. This age group was also allowed play matches, but again only with teams from their own sports club. The competition was therefore also halted here. For adults over twenty-seven, stricter measures apply. They were allowed to play sports outside with a maximum of two people at a distance of 1.5 m, but for outdoor sports at sports

203. This chapter was created in with the assistance of Ms. N. van Abeelen, legal assistant at De Voort lawyers | mediators. It previously appeared in the Tijdschrift voor Sport & recht, edition 2-3 2021.

facilities or at a location (on the initiative of the municipality) a maximum number of four people applies. In addition, this group was not allowed to play matches.

The measures mentioned above applied to amateur athletes only. Top athletes could, since December 2020, train and play matches if they participated in top sports competitions. However, there must be training sessions and matches of institutions for top-level sport. A select group was made in consultation with the Dutch sports organization NOC*NSF and the Dutch soccer association KNVB for all top athletes with a status, top sports competitions and footballers from the Eredivisie and first division. This included approximately 1,000 soccer players and 5,000 athletes from other sports (field hockey, basketball, water polo, volleyball, handball, korfball, beach volleyball, baseball, softball, rugby, ice hockey, wheelchair basketball, indoor soccer, cricket, badminton and table tennis).[204]The medical staff of the NOC*NSF has recommended that the athletes and coaches of the Dutch team should travel to the Tokyo Olympic and Paralympic Games in the summer vaccinated. For now, the athletes will only be called upon to do so based on their behaviour, compliance with protocols and the need for regular testing, among other things. It was[205] announced that the athletes who will be delegated to Tokyo could be vaccinated on a priority basis.[206]

In April 2021, the Dutch government started allowing events and activities where visitors have to bring a test certificate. Visitors must undergo a quick test for corona before they can enter. With a negative result from that test, they will receive a test certificate that must be shown at the entrance to the event. These rapid testing pilots are also being used at various sporting events, including elite sports competitions. The goal of these pilots is to open various sectors earlier. To this end, the government is investigating whether visitors have confidence in the safety of events and activities, what the experience is for visitors to get tested in advance, what the experience is for organizations to check for a valid negative test certificate, whether the supporting digital framework and apps work well and whether the purpose-built test lanes function properly. However, the same corona measures will continue to apply during these pilots, such as keeping 1.5 m distance.[207] At this moment spectators must show a QR-code upon entry to show they are either vaccinated or recently tested.

Financial Support Measures by the Dutch Government

237. Both the Dutch government and various sports federations and organizations have taken support measures to provide financial support to the sports sector. This way, sports associations can continue to represent and offer sports both during and after the corona pandemic. In January 2021, the government still announced that the sports sector would be hit hard by the extension of the corona pandemic

204. 'Corona and sport', central government.co.uk.
205. 'Top sport and vaccination against Covid-19', nocnsf.co.uk.
206. https://www.rijksoverheid.nl/onderwerpen/coronavirus-vaccinatie/volgorde-van-vaccinatie-tegen-het-coronavirus/volgorde-vaccinatie-voor-mensen-die-niet-in-de-zorg-werken.
207. 'Pilots test for event access', rijksoverheid.nl.

measures. Because the Dutch sports infrastructure – which is supported by associations and volunteers – is under pressure, sector-specific support is needed to ensure that the sports sector can once again make its contribution to keeping the Dutch population fit and resilient after the corona measures. The government therefore decided to extend several support measures for the sports sector that had been initiated for 2020 until 30 June 2021 (TASO scheme, Tegemoetkoming Verhuur sport accommodations, Specific allowance for ice rinks and swimming pools). A total of EUR 240 million was made available for this package of measures.[208]These support measures, together with other important support measures by the Dutch government, will be briefly discussed here.

The NOW Scheme

238. One of the most important support measures of the Dutch government is the NOW scheme (the Temporary Emergency Measure for Bridging Employment). This measure supports companies and (sports) associations in paying staff. With this, the government takes on a substantial part of the wage bill. The purpose of the scheme is to help employers pay the wage costs in the event of an (expected) acute loss of turnover of at least 20% for a period of three months due to a reduction in business activity caused by extraordinary circumstances that cannot reasonably be considered part of the normal business risk. This aid enables companies and associations to retain employees for the hours they worked before the downturn. As a result, as many jobs as possible are preserved. The scheme sees under 'extraordinary circumstances' the outbreak of COVID-19, but this may also include other calamities.[209]The compensation – which can be applied for at the UWV – amounts to a maximum of 85% of the wage bill. Participation in the NOW scheme is subject to the condition that the employer has an obligation to make an effort to keep the wage bill as stable as possible. In addition, the employer is expected not to request dismissal of his employees for economic reasons during the period for which the subsidy is granted.[210]In the meantime, the scheme has been extended twice with different application deadlines.[211]

239. In the sports sector, too, the NOW scheme can help with wage costs. Because of the various measures and several training sessions and matches being halted or having been halted, the sports sector is also experiencing difficulties in paying, for example, trainers and maintenance staff. There is little income coming

208. Parliamentary letter extending economic support and recovery package, *Parliamentary Papers II* 2020/21, 35420, No. AB, p. 19.
209. P.A. Hogewind-Wolters and S.F.H. Jellinghaus, '*The Short Road from Working Time Reduction to NOW: Speed over Perfection?*', TAP 2020/95, issue 3, p. 6. *See also* P.A. Hogewind-Wolters & S.F.H. Jellinghaus, *NOW 2.0: Final Chord or Prelude?*, TAP 2020/159, A.M. Helstone, '*From WTV to NOW; from Working Time Reduction to Wage Subsidy*', ArbeidsRecht 2020/22 and J.M. van Slooten, '*The NOW: A Wage Subsidy Scheme with Some Strategic Aspects*', Ondernemingsrecht 2020/XII.
210. P.A. Hogewind-Wolters and S.F.H. Jellinghaus, '*The Short Road from Working Time Reduction to NOW: Speed over Perfection?*', TAP 2020/95, issue 3, p. 9.
211. For a current overview, *see* NOW as well as P.A. Hogewind-Wolters & S.F.H. Jellinghaus, *Corona in: SDU Opmaat Labor Law+*, updated to 14 Apr. 2021.

in and the staff often cannot be put to work. The regulation can help sports associations, sports entrepreneurs, event organizers and professional sports organizations to overcome the crisis.[212]However, in practice, it appears that the regulation does not support everyone. As mentioned, one is only eligible for the regulation when there is at least a 20% loss of turnover over a period of three months. Many revenues, such as membership fees and sponsorships, have already come in at the beginning of the season. As a result, the minimum loss of 20% in the months for which an allowance is claimed is not always achieved. Furthermore, salaries are often paid through a sports service organization. Because the personnel costs are not paid via the club's payroll tax number, the club itself is not eligible for the scheme. The sports service organization is also not eligible for the NOW scheme, since it itself does not readily meet the requirement of at least a 20% drop in turnover. Even though these problems have been raised with politicians, no solutions have yet been found.[213]

The TASO Scheme

240. In addition to the NOW scheme, the government has also made the TASO scheme (Tegemoetkoming amateur sports organizations COVID-19). The purpose of this scheme is to limit the financial damage experienced by amateur sports organizations. This is primarily to prevent them from collapsing in the short term due to the immediate financial effects of the corona crisis and secondarily to ensure that these organizations remain capable of making investments in the quality of the sports on offer in the longer term. The scheme is intended for amateur sports organizations that have suffered at least a 10% loss of turnover in the quarter in question for which compensation is sought. In addition, there must have been financial loss of at least EUR 1,500.00. The loss must be the result of the measures taken to combat COVID-19. It is an allowance for the fixed costs of sports clubs that are not eligible for the Tegemoetkoming Vaste Lasten (TVL) and/or have not been compensated for salary costs through the NOW scheme. The fixed costs for self-owned or managed accommodation, club dues, uncompensated personnel costs and the canteen result are among the factors taken into account when determining the concession. The compensation depends on the financial loss and amounts to a maximum of EUR 12,500.00.[214]

The TVL Scheme

241. As just mentioned, there is also the TVL scheme. This scheme concerns an allowance for the fixed costs of an enterprise, including a sports club. In order to qualify for the allowance, the company must have lost at least 30% of its turnover and have at least EUR 1,500 of fixed costs per quarter. The fixed costs for the Sport and Recreation sector are determined at 34% of the turnover. The allowance

212. 'Overview of financial support measures for associations', KNVB 2020, p. 1.
213. 'Overview of financial support measures for associations', KNVB 2020, pp. 1–2.
214. Policy Rule on concessions for amateur sports organizations and landlords of sports facilities COVID-19 (*Government Gazette* 2021, 4754).

amounts to a maximum of 85% of the fixed costs, up to a maximum of EUR 330,000.[215]The allowance can be applied for a period of three months at a time.[216] It is not possible to use both the TASO regulation and the TVL regulation. However, it has become apparent that many clubs initially applied for the TVL regulation, while they later found out that the TASO regulation would be better for them. It has been agreed with the Ministry of Health, Welfare and Sport that these associations can fill out that they did not apply for the TVL regulation when they apply for the TASO regulation, which means that they can still qualify for the TASO regulation. They will then have the opportunity to repay the TVL subsidy until it is determined.[217]

The TVS Scheme

242. For landlords of sports accommodations, the government has created the TVS scheme (Tegemoetkoming verhuurders sportaccommodaties COVID-19). This scheme is intended to waive the rent of a sports accommodation when this accommodation cannot be used by amateur sports organizations due to corona measures. Because rental costs can be substantial for sports clubs, the government has devised this scheme with the aim of encouraging landlords to waive (part of) the rent for sports clubs. The relief is requested by the landlord (municipality, sports company or private landlord) who has waived (part of) the rent due to forced closure of the organization by the corona measures. It only concerns remission of rent to tenants who meet the definition of an amateur sports organization. Many sports clubs use a non-utility rent. In this case the rent is not dependent on the extent to which the accommodation is actually used. In this case a maximum of 45% of the lost rent is compensated. When making use of user fees, where an accommodation is rented per hour or part of the day that it is actually used, the full 100% of the lost rent is compensated.[218]

The Specific Allowance for Swimming Pools and Ice Rinks

243. A government support measure for a specific sports sector is the Specific Allowance for Swimming Pools and Ice Rinks. Municipalities and operators of swimming pools and ice rinks have done everything in their power to keep these facilities open, but because of the corona measures this was not economically viable. As a result, swimming pools and ice rinks were unable to receive visitors for a long time, while a large part of their business is based on turnover from large-scale visitors.[219] To mitigate the financial consequences, a sum of EUR 100 million

---

215. 'Contribution to Fixed Charges (TVL)', nocnsf.co.uk.
216. 'Tegemoetkoming Vasteasten (TVL)', rvo.nl.
217. 'Financial compensation for sports clubs: applications for TASO for Q4 possible until 5 April', nocnsf.nl.
218. Policy Rule on concessions for amateur sports organizations and landlords of sports facilities COVID-19 (*Government Gazette* 2021, 4754).
219. Regulation on specific payment of swimming pools and ice rinks COVID-19 (*Government Gazette* 2021, 14868).

has been made available for 2020 and EUR 80 million for the first half of 2021.[220] The scheme prevents the closure of swimming pools and ice rinks. According to the scheme, the Minister may, upon application by a municipality, provide the benefit to compensate for the operating deficit faced by a swimming pool or ice rink.[221]

The TOGS Scheme

244. Brief attention to the Tegemoetkoming Ondernemers Get getroffen Sectoren COVID-19 (TOGS) is also in order in this contribution. Although this allowance can no longer be applied for, the scheme has provided important support to sports associations. The TOGS was created as an emergency measure to support entrepreneurs during the corona crisis. Entrepreneurs, including sports organizations, who were directly affected by various government measures to contain the coronavirus, could receive a one-time compensation of EUR 4,000.00 in the period from the end of March to the end of June 2020.[222] However, there were a number of conditions for this, including the requirement for a physical location such as a sports canteen. In addition, the expected turnover decrease of that period had to be at least EUR 4,000.00, as well as the expected fixed costs of that same period.[223] Several sports associations could also apply for this concession.

Tax Relief for Online Classes

245. When exercising in a sports facility, the low tax rate of 9% applies. Because the corona measures entail a mandatory closure of gyms, many gyms and entrepreneurs offer online sports lessons.[224]Gyms and entrepreneurs offering online sports lessons have been given a temporary reduced VAT rate on these sports lessons until the mandatory closure of gyms is lifted.[225]

Financial Support Measures from the Sports Sector

246. In addition to the fact that the Dutch government has made various arrangements to financially support the sports sector, sports federations and organizations have also taken financial measures. Some of these measures will be outlined here.

The Corona Emergency Fund for Sports

247. The Dutch sports organization NOC*NSF has established a Corona Emergency Fund for Sports partly with the support of the Dutch Lottery. The fund set

220. 'Specific Allowance for Ice Rinks and Swimming Pools', www.dus-i.nl.
221. Regulation on specific payment of swimming pools and ice rinks COVID-19 (*Government Gazette* 2021, 14868).
222. 'Tegemoetkoming Ondernemers Get affected Sectoren Covid-19', rijksoverheid.nl.
223. 'Emergency desk for entrepreneurs also for sports associations and entrepreneurs in sport', nocnsf.co.uk.
224. 'Overview of support and recovery package', rijksoverheid.nl.
225. Parliamentary letter extending economic support and recovery package, *Parliamentary Papers II* 2020/21, 35420, No. AB, p. 14.

aside funds to help the national sports infrastructure get through the crisis. It was meant as a kind of safety net for sports associations that would get into current payment problems because of the corona crisis. The emergency fund supported sports federations and sports associations in 2020, but will also continue to strengthen the financial position of sports federations in 2021.[226]

Suspend Repayment for Business Credit

248. Stichting Waarborgfonds Sport (SWS), a foundation with the objective of stimulating sports organizations to own high-quality accommodations, has decided together with several banks at the beginning of the corona pandemic that small- and medium-sized enterprises, including sports associations, can suspend their repayment for six months for business loans up to EUR 2.5 million. This is subject to the condition that the association is financially healthy and does not already have payment problems.[227]However, the various banks regulate themselves how deferment should be requested.[228]

The Guarantee of Emergency Credit by the SWS

249. In order to cope with liquidity problems, sports clubs and organizations can apply to their banks for a temporary loan: the Emergency Loan. The bank will often ask for a guarantee for this, because they want certainty that the loan will be paid back. SWS can arrange this guarantee for the emergency loan upon request.[229] It applies to sports clubs and sports organizations that are in liquidity problems due to the corona measures of the government. The emergency loan can be used, for example, to bridge the period until a requested subsidy is paid out or it can be used to absorb the financial damage caused by COVID-19 and spread it over the coming years.[230]

Support Measures by the KNVB

250. The KNVB has made several financial support measures to support the soccer sector during the corona pandemic. This included a financial support package for soccer clubs. The support was created by the main sponsor ING bank, the Orange players and the KNVB. The package consists of a combination of donations, measures and concessions totalling EUR 11 million. The package is intended for both paid soccer clubs and amateur clubs.[231] Furthermore, several small measures have been taken including the non-execution of a number of monthly direct debits to the KNVB, the reduction of certain costs and the refund of, for example,

226. 'Extra support for sports federations', nocnsf.co.uk.
227. 'Overview of financial support measures for clubs', KNVB, p. 2.
228. 'Banks and SWS give sports clubs "air" with postponement of repayment obligations', sws.co.uk.
229. 'Apply for Deposit Emergency Credit', sws.co.uk.
230. 'Deposit Emergency Credit through Guarantee Fund Sport Foundation (SWS), nocnsf.co.uk.
231. 'Overview of financial support measures for clubs', KNVB, p. 2.

match fees.[232] In addition, the KNVB made an incentive budget available for soccer clubs to apply for. The budget was intended to organize soccer offers at clubs or to bind existing and/or new target groups to the clubs. The stimulation budget enabled all kinds of soccer activities to be started.[233]

Paid Soccer Agreement

251. On 7 May 2020, the employers' organization Federation of Professional Football Organizations (FBO), players' unions Association of Dutch Professional Football Players (VVCS) and ProProf and professional association Coaches Professional Football (CBV) reached an agreement in professional soccer in which collective agreements are made regarding the reduction of salaries with a potential size of approximately EUR 35 million. In addition to binding agreements, this includes guidelines until 1 January 2021. It concerns:[234]

Guideline:

- Refraining from, or finding an amicable arrangement with respect to, collective bonuses;
- a reduction in salary on the basis of a progressive graduated scale. Starting at 2.5% for annual salaries over €25,000 gross and increasing to a maximum of 20%, whereby the parties have agreed to take government measures into account;
- waiving any remaining vacation days for the 2019/2020 season;
- The option of paying the vacation allowance for the 2019/2020 season in the month of June instead of May.

The binding agreements see:

- The interim opening and extension of the Collective Agreement for Contract Players in Professional Football from July 1, 2020 to June 30, 2023;
- A reduction in the mandatory number of contract players in the First Division, from 16 to 14 in 2020/2021 and to 15 in 2021/2022;
- A reduction in the testing limit regarding vacation allowance for contract players in the 2020/2021 and 2021/2022 seasons;
- The waiver by the players' unions of an increase in the employer contribution rate effective 1 January 2021;
- Keeping the income criterion for non-EU players the same if possible (as set for the 2019/2020 season).
- Duration of salary reduction.

---

232. 'Overview of financial support measures for clubs', KNVB, p. 3.
233. 'KNVB incentive budget fully deployed', knvb.nl.
234. https://fbo.nl/2020/05/07/uniek-akkoord-betaald-voetbal/.

Future

252. For now, the COVID-19 pandemic is not at its end. The decline of hospitalization of COVID-19 infected patient led to a scale down of measures for sports. It is however not yet clear to what extend these scales downs will continue.

During the corona crisis, a lot of financial relief measures have been taken by the government and the sports sector. Most of the applications for relief from the government will have to be submitted by June 2021. After that the schemes have been downsized.

Selected Bibliography

Branco Martins, R. 'De eerste Europese CLA in de sport'. FBO (2002) en M.J.

Bungener, A.F. & E. Verhulp. 'De eenzijdige verlengingsoptie in de arbeidsovereenkomst'. *Arbeidsrecht,* No. 64 (2004).

Clarijs, C.P.J. & S.F.H. Jellinghaus. 'Kroniek van het Sportrecht 2004–2005'. *Anton Magazine/Sportzaken,* No. 1 (2005): 10–15.

Hendrickx, F. 'Vrijheid en stabiliteit in voetbalcontracten'. SMA (2003): 61 ff.

Jellinghaus, S.F.H. (ed.). 'Buiten rechte of buiten spel'. *Jonge Balie congresbundel* (Paris, 2008).

Jellinghaus, S.F.H. 'Het opleidings-en solidariteitssysteem van de FIFA: de stand van zaken'. *arbeidsrechtelijke annotaties,* No. 2 (2005): blz. 4 ft.

Jellinghaus, S.F.H. *Introductie in het sportrecht* (Arbeid Integraal, 2003), 70 ft.

Jellinghaus, S.F.H. (ed.), *Capita Sportrecht,* Antwerpen/'s-Hertogenbosch: Gompel & Scavina 2021.

Kollen, F.C. *Sport en Recht* (Deventer: Kluwer, 2004), 704 ff.

Maessen. 'Europees sociale dialoog voor betaald voetbal'. *Arbeid Integraal* (2003): 100 ff.

Nieuwland, D.S. 'De eenzijdige optie nader beschouwd'. *Rechtshulp* 6, No. 7 (2004): 37 ff.

Schwartz, D. & Hahn, G.A., 'Een introductie tot het tuchtrechtelijk proces in het waterpolo', *Tijdschrift voor Sport en Recht*, 2020, 1/2.

Schwartz, D., 'Loondoorbetalingsplicht bij geschorste sporters. Tuchtrechtelijke schorsingen *all in the game?' Tijdschrift voor Sport en Recht*, 2020, ½.

Siekmann, R.C.R. & N.J.P. Giltay Veth (eds). 'De afschaffing van het transfersysteem in het betaald voetbal (de zaak Bosman)'. *De Vrieseborch* (1996): 9 ff.

Van der Burg c.s., H.H. *Sport en recht* (Zwolle: Hessenpoort, 1992).

Van Staveren, H.T. & P.T. Verloren van Themaat. De verhouding van het vergoedingenstelsel van het Nederlandse betaald voetbal met het Nederlandse recht en het Europees recht (Utrecht: Den Haag, 1979), 27 ff.

Van Staveren, H.T. 'Het nieuwe ontslagrecht: verminderde mogelijkheden voor het "alternatieve transfersysteem"', AA (1998): 660 ff.

Van Staveren, H.T. 'Sportwetgeving op nationaal niveau gewenst?'. *Notitie naar aanleiding van de motie Rijpstra/Middel* (Amsterdam: Vrije Universiteit Amsterdam, 5 September 2003).

Van Staveren, H.T. *Het voetbalcontract* (Kluwer, 1980), 21 ff.

Van Staveren, H.T. *Op de grens van sportregel en rechtsregel* (Amsterdam: Oratie Vrije Universiteit Amsterdam, 1992; Deventer: Kluwer, 1992).

Selected Bibliography

Van Staveren, H.T. *Sport en Recht* (Nieuwegein: Arko sports Media, 2007). *Tijdschrift voor Sport en recht* (Paris: Uitgeverij Paris, (4x P.Y))

Index

The numbers here refer to paragraph numbers.

Index

Index

www.ingramcontent.com/pod-product-compliance
Lightning Source LLC
Chambersburg PA
CBHW071351230926
51846CB00002B/509
9789403541259